Primitive Christian Symbols

by JEAN DANIÉLOU, S.J.

Translated by DONALD ATTWATER

BALTIMORE · HELICON PRESS

This is a translation of Les Symboles chrétiens primitifs (*Éditions du Seuil, Paris, 1961*).

246.2
D 148

© Éditions du Seuil 1961
English translation © Burns and Oates Ltd., 1964

Made and printed in Great Britain by
Spottiswoode Ballantyne and Co. Ltd., London and Colchester for
Helicon Press Inc.
1120 North Calvert Street
Baltimore, Maryland 21202

Contents

Illustrations

between pp. 88 and 89

1. Axe scratched on stone ossuary, from cemetery of Dominus Flevit, Jerusalem

2. Cross in form of axe, found near the Great Theatre, Ephesus

3. Six-pointed cross or star on cover of stone ossuary

4. Two-horned cross on stone found at Pool of Bethesda, Jerusalem

5 & 6. Ploughs scratched on ossuaries, from Dominus Flevit

7. Whale (?) in the sea: graffito from Dominus Flevit

8–12. Stelae from cemetery at Khirbet Kilkis, near Hebron

13. Part of the inscriptions in the tomb of Nur at Beth-phage

14. Cross combined with Tree of Life or palm branch: mosaic from Beth ha-Shitta

15. Tree of Life, from Dominus Flevit

Acknowledgement

The illustrations are reproduced by courtesy of Tipografia dei Padri Francescani, Jerusalem, and of P. B. Bagatti, who took all the photographs except Nos. 1 and 13.

Introduction

Before it spread in the Greek and Roman world, and adopted its language and imagery, Christianity had a first period in which its environment was Jewish and its language Aramaic. This Judaic Christianity had no future, and the traces of it had almost disappeared, but forgotten works that had been preserved in Eastern languages, Armenian, Syriac, Coptic, Ethiopic, have gradually enabled its literary heritage to be restored: such writings as the *Odes of Solomon*, the *Ascension of Isaias*, the *Testaments of the Twelve Patriarchs*, and others. In another book, *Théologie du judéo-christianisme* (Paris, Desclée, 1958), I have tried to recover the relevant mentality. This belongs to the spiritual and imaginative world of Jewish apocalyptic writing: it is a theology of history, set out by means of symbols.

This study led me to ask myself whether some of the images bequeathed to us by Christian antiquity did not go back to this primitive period; whether their meaning and significance must not be looked for there. From 1954 onwards I published the results of these researches in various periodicals, and it is these studies, revised and finished off, that are collected in this book. In them I recorded the unexpectedness of the symbols of the cross, particularly the plough symbol, and gave recognition to the importance of the crown in sacramental symbolism.

I was surprised to find baptism compared to a chariot in which man is carried up to Heaven. Moreover, I was led to the conclusion that certain better-known symbols, that of the fish especially, could have other significances than the ones usually given to them.

The general unexpectedness of these conclusions left me in a state of perplexity. What, then, was the interest with which I read, in the *Osservatore Romano* of 6 August 1960, an article by one of the best Palestinian archaeologists, Father B. Bagatti: in it he reported surprising finds at Hebron, Nazareth and Jerusalem, which had uncovered a number of ossuaries and funerary steles of unquestionably Judaeo-Christian character, which clearly displayed most of the symbols which I had already identified as Judaeo-Christian in the literary remains. There are the plough and the palm, the star and the growing plant, the cross and the fish. These ossuaries belonged to a Judaeo-Christian community existing in Palestine at the end of the first century and into the second. The symbols thereon have been studied by Father E. Testa in a thesis upheld at the Biblical Institute in Rome.[1] This work had not yet been published when I wrote this book, and I knew of it only from what is said about it in Father Bagatti's article, and from what Father Testa himself wrote in the *Osservatore Romano* of 25 September 1960.

So it has now become possible to write a new page in the history of Christianity. Up till now, nothing has been more obscure than the period between the Church's very beginnings, as narrated in St Paul's letters and in the Acts of the Apostles, and her development in the Graeco-Roman world, at Alexandria, at Carthage and at Rome.

[1] *Il Simbolismo dei Giudei-Cristiani* (Jerusalem, 1962).

Light is beginning to shine on this dark age. And what everybody can see now is precisely the importance at that time of this Christianity of Semitic build, which we did not suspect and some of whose characteristics are revealed by the study of Judaeo-Christian symbolism.

ABBREVIATIONS IN REFERENCES TO PERIODICALS, COLLECTIONS, ETC.

A.C.	Antike und Christentum.
B.K.V.	Bibliothek der Kirchenväter.
C.B.Q.	Catholic Biblical Quarterly.
C.D.C.	Damascus Fragments.
C.R.A.I.B.L.	Comptes rendus de l'Académie des Inscriptions et Belles Lettres.
C.S.E.L.	Corpus Scriptorum Ecclesiasticorum Latinorum.
D.A.C.L.	Dictionnaire d'archéologie chrétienne et de liturgie.
D.A.G.R.	Dictionnaire des antiquités grecques et romaines.
D.S.D.	Manual of Discipline.
D.S.H.	Midrash of Habacuc.
D.S.S.	Dead Sea Scrolls.
D.S.T.	Collection of Hymns.
D.S.W.	War of the Sons of Light against the Sons of Darkness.
E.L.	Ephemerides Liturgicae.
E.T.	Evangelische Theologie.
E.T.L.	Ephemerides Theologicae Lovanienses.
F.H.G.	Fragmenta Historicorum Graecorum.
G.C.S.	Griechische christliche Schriftsteller.
H.T.R.	Harvard Theological Review.
J.B.L.	Journal of Biblical Literature.
J.T.S.	Journal of Theological Studies.
M.G.W.J.	Monatschrift für Geschichte und Wissenschaft des Judentums.
N.T.S.	New Testament Studies.
P.E.Q.	Palestine Exploration Quarterly.
P.G.	Patrologia Graeca.
P.L.	Patrologia Latina.
P.O.	Patrologia Orientalis.
I Q. Ben.	Qumran Cave I, Benedictions.
I Q. Test.	Qumran Cave I, Testimonia.
IV Q. Flor.	Qumran Cave IV, Florilegium.
R.B.	Revue biblique.
Rev. Bén.	Revue bénédictine.
R.E.G.	Revue des Études grecques.

R.O.C.	Revue de l'Orient chrétien.
R.S.R.	Recherches de Science religieuse.
R.T.	Revue thomiste.
S.C.	Sources chrétiennes.
S.D.B.	Supplement to the Dictionnaire de la Bible.
T.W.N.T.	Theologisches Wörterbuch zum Neuen Testament.
V.C.	Vigiliae Christianae.
V.D.	Verbum Domini.
Z.K.T.	Zeitschrift für katholische Theologie.
Z.R.G.G.	Zeitschrift für Religions- und Geistesgeschichte.

CONTRACTIONS IN REFERENCES TO ANCIENT WORKS

AMBROSE
Sacram.: On the Sacraments.
De Helia et jejunio: On Elias and Fasting.
Exp. Luc: Expositions of Luke.
Myst.: On the Mysteries.

APOSTOLIC CONSTITUTIONS
Const. Apost.

ASTERIUS THE SOPHIST
Hom.: Homilies on the Psalms.

AUGUSTINE
En. Psalm.: Expositions of the Psalms.
Epist.: Letters.
Tract. Joh.: Treatise on St John.

CASSIAN
Coll.: Conferences.

CLEMENT OF ALEXANDRIA
Exc. Theod.: Extracts from Theodotus.
Paed.: Pedagogue.
Protrept.: Exhortation to the Gentiles.
Quis dives: What Rich Man shall be Saved?
Strom.: Stromata.

CYPRIAN
Epist.: Letters.
Test.: Testimonia.

CYRIL OF JERUSALEM
Catech.: Catecheses.
Paral.: On the Paralytic Man.
Procatech.: Procatecheses.

DIDYMUS
Com. Psalm.: Commentary on the Psalms.
Trin.: On the Trinity.

EPHRAEM
Hymn. Epiph.: Hymn on the Epiphany.
Hymn. Parad.: Hymn on Paradise (Beck).

Epiphanius
  Pan.: Medicine Box.

Eusebius
  Com. Psalm.: Commentary on the Psalms.
  Hist. eccl.: Church History.
  Onom.: Onomasticon.
  Dem. ev.: Demonstration of the Gospel.

Eutropius
  De solst. et aequinoct.: On the Solstice and the Equinox.

Gaudentius of Brescia
  Serm.: Sermons.

Gregory of Elvira
  De fide orth.: On the Orthodox Faith.
  Tract.: Treatises.

Gregory Nazianzen
  Or.: Sermons.

Gregory of Nyssa
  Asc. Chr.: On the Ascension of Christ.
  In Cant.: On the Song of Songs.
  De an. et res.: On the Soul and the Resurrection.
  Ep.: Letters.
  In bapt.: On Baptism.
  Laud. Bas.: Panegyric on his Brother Basil.
  Virg.: On Virginity.
  Beat.: On the Beatitudes.

Hermas
  Mand.: Precepts.
  Sim.: Parables.

Hippolytus
  Ben. Isaac, Jac., Mos.: On the Benedictions of Isaac, Jacob and Moses.
  Com. Dan.: Commentary on Daniel.
  Com. Cant.: Commentary on the Song of Songs.
  Elench.: Refutation of heresies.

Ignatius of Antioch
  Eph.: Letter to the Ephesians.
  Philad.: Letter to the Philadelphians.
  Trall.: Letter to the Trallians.

Irenaeus
  Adv. haer.: Against Heresies.
  Dem.: Presentation of the Apostolic Preaching.

Contractions

JEROME
 Com. Is.: Commentary on Isaias.
 Com. Mat.: Commentary on Matthew.
 Com. Zach.: Commentary on Zacharias.

JOHN CHRYSOSTOM
 Hom. Eliam: Homily on Elias.
 Hom. Phil.: Homily on the Epistle to the Philippians.

JULIAN THE APOSTATE
 Disc.: Discourses.

JUSTIN
 I Apol.: First Apology.
 Dial.: Dialogue with Trypho.

LACTANTIUS
 Div. inst.: Divinae Institutiones.

MAXIMUS OF TURIN
 Hom.: Homilies.

MAXIMUS OF TYRE
 Disc.: Discourses.

METHODIUS OF OLYMPUS
 Conv.: Symposium of the Ten Virgins.
 Res.: On the Resurrection.

NILUS
 Monast. exercit.: The Monastic Exercise.

OPTATUS OF MILEVIS
 Schism. Donat.: On the Donatist Schism.

ORIGEN
 Com. Gen.: Commentary on Genesis.
 Com. Joh.: Commentary on John.
 Com. Mat.: Commentary on Matthew.
 Com. Rom.: Commentary on the Epistle to the Romans.
 Contra Cels.: Against Celsus.
 De Or.: On Prayer.
 Hom. Ezech.: Homily on Ezechiel.
 Hom. Num.: Homily on Numbers.

PHILO
 Her.: On the Heir of Divine Things.
 Opif.: On the Creation.
 Praem.: On Rewards.
 Quaest. Gen., Ex.: Questions on Genesis, Exodus.

Spec. leg.: Particular Laws.
Vita Mos.: Life of Moses.

PSEUDO-CLEMENT
Hom.: Homilies.
Rec.: Recognitiones.

PSEUDO-JEROME
Com. Marc.: Commentary on Mark.

PSEUDO-PLUTARCH
Vita Hom.: Life of Homer.

SIBYLLINE ORACLES
Or. Sib.

TACITUS
Hist.: Histories.

TATIAN
Disc.: Discourses.

TERTULLIAN
Adv. Jud.: Against the Jews.
Anim.: On the Soul.
Bapt.: On Baptism.
De idol.: On Idolatry.

TESTAMENT OF ABRAHAM
Test. Abr.

THEODORET
Quaest. Ex.: Questions on Exodus.

ZENO OF VERONA
Tract.: Treatises.

I

The Palm and the Crown

The New Testament does not destroy the Old—it is the fulfilment of it. There is no more remarkable example of this principle than that provided by liturgical feasts. The great solemnities of Judaism, the Passover and Pentecost, have remained the great solemnities of Christianity, but bearing a new meaning. There is, however, apparently an exception, provided by the feast of Tabernacles, the *Skenopegia* of the Septuagint, which took place in September. There is only one remaining vestige of this in the Roman liturgy, the lesson from Leviticus about it, read on the Ember Saturday in September. It is natural to ask if the feast has not left other traces in Christian liturgy and exegesis.[1] But before examining that question we have to look into the feast's significance at the time of Christ.

The ultimate origin of the feast of Tabernacles is to be found in the cycle of seasonal feasts. It was the feast of the vintage, as Pentecost was of the grain harvest.[2] This is indicated by the very passage of Leviticus (23. 39-43) that prescribes the celebration, and Philo emphasizes this aspect (*Spec. leg.*, II, 204). The characteristic observances of the feast have reference to its seasonal character: the

---

[1] Cf. J. Daniélou, "Les Quatre-Temps de septembre et la fête des Tabernacles", in *La Maison-Dieu*, 46 (1956), pp. 114-36; "La fête des Tabernacles dans l'exégèse patristique", in *Studia Patristica*, I (Berlin, 1957), pp. 262-79.

[2] J. Pedersen, *Israel*, III-IV (London, 1940), pp. 418-25; H. J. Kraus, *Gottesdienst in Israel* (Munich, 1954); J. van Goudoever, *Biblical Calendars* (Leiden, 1959), pp. 30-5.

I

living for seven days in arbours (σκηναί) made of branches, the libations of water to obtain rain, the procession round the altar on the eighth day, when each person carried in his right hand a nosegay (*lulab*) of willow, myrtle and palm, and in his left a citron (*ethrog*).[3]

But, as in other feasts having a similar origin, Jewish thought wove the memory of an historical event into the recurring seasonal festival. The Passover, feast of the first-fruits and of unleavened bread, became the feast of the first-born who were spared (*passah*) by the destroying angel. Pentecost was associated with the giving of the Law on Sinai. And so with the feast of Tabernacles. Leviticus itself explains (23. 43) that it is intended to remind the Jews of their sojourn in tents (σκηναί) in the wilderness at the time of the Exodus. This interpretation belongs to the priestly tradition. It is found in Philo (*Spec. leg.*, II, 204), in the rabbinic tradition,[4] and in the Fathers of the Church.[5]

But, beginning with the prophets and above all in the period after the exile, past events in Israel's history, especially the Exodus, were recalled in order to keep up the people's hope in future events, in which Yahweh's power would be manifested in favour of his own still more strikingly: the events of the Exodus became the figures of eschatological realities. This was the beginning of typology. It is true of the Passover and the going out from Egypt—they were seen as the figure of the eschatological deliverance of God's people—but it is eminently true of the feast of Tabernacles, which more than any other

[3] See Strack-Billerbeck, *Kommentar zum N.T.*, II, pp. 774–812.
[4] *Ibid.*, p. 778.
[5] Theodoret, *Quaest. Ex.*, 54 (*P.G.*, 80, 276B–C); Jerome, *Com. Zach.*, 3, 14 (*P.L.*, 25, 1536).

festival took on eschatological significance. Perhaps one reason for this may be found in the fact that, as Philo points out (*loc. cit.*), the feast of Tabernacles marks the end (τελείωσις) of the year's agrarian cycle.[6]

But there is an older and deeper reason, namely, that the feast appears to have a very special connection with messianic hopes. The origins of the link are not clear. But the feast of Tabernacles would seem to be related to the annual festival of the setting up of the kingdom, or rather (as Kraus thinks), to the renewal of the Covenant by the Davidic king. Scattered fragments of the feast may exist in the three great Jewish feasts of the month Tishri, *Rosh-hash-Shanah*, *Kippur* and *Sukkoth* (σκηναί)[7]; and it could have taken on a messianic character in Judaism, being brought into relation with the expectation of the king to come. A festival originating in seasonal rites would then have undergone a transformation during the epoch of the kings, new elements being introduced into it.

In any case it is certain that several texts bear witness to the importance after the exile of the feast of Tabernacles in connection with messianic expectancy. The first of them is the last chapter of Zacharias. First we see Yahweh standing upon "the Mount of Olives, which is over against Jerusalem, toward the east" (14. 4). Then it is said that "living waters shall go out from Jerusalem" (14. 8). And, most particularly, we are told that the remnant of the nations that came against Jerusalem shall come there once a year to keep the feast of Tabernacles (14. 16). The feast would thus be seen as a figure of the messianic kingdom. The other two texts seem to refer

---

[6] Theodoret (*loc. cit.*) calls it the feast of consummation (συντελείας) at the year's end.

[7] N. H. Snaith, *The Jewish New Year Festival* (London, 1947), pp. 75–80.

to the feast too: the flow of water recalls one of its ritual observances, and the Mount of Olives is the place where the branches for the arbours were cut.[8] This last point will have its own interest when we have to bring together Jesus' entry into Jerusalem, coming from the Mount of Olives, and the feast of Tabernacles.

Furthermore, there is a psalm of clearly messianic character which has a place in the post-exilic liturgy of the feast. This is Psalm 117, which was sung during the procession on the eighth day, when the Jews went round the altar carrying the *lulab*. It is to this procession that verse 27 alludes: "*Constituite diem sollemnem in condensis usque ad cornu altaris*". Now this psalm refers to the Messiah as one who is to come: "*Benedictus qui venit in nomine Domini*" (verse 26); and it hails his coming with the cry: "*Hosanna* – Save me!" (verse 25). This psalm contains, too, another messianic text that the New Testament applies to Christ: "The very stone which the builders rejected has become the chief stone at the corner" (verse 22). All these passages show that the liturgy of Tabernacles was a very special occasion of messianic expectation.

The messianic interpretation of the feast in Judaism was continued into the early Christian centuries. Commenting on Zacharias 14. 16, St Jerome explains that, "through a fallacious hope", the Jews saw in the feast of Tabernacles "a figure of things to come at the millennium" (3. 14; *P.L.*, 25, 1536A). They interpreted the stream of living waters and the rebuilding of Jerusalem in the same way (1529A). Thus the festivities of Tabernacles, when each

---

[8] See 2 Esdras [Neh.] 8. 15: "Go forth to the mount, and fetch branches . . . to make tabernacles."

man ate and drank with his family in his arbour decked with greenery, appeared to the Jews as a prefiguring of material pleasures in the messianic kingdom. The messianic hopes fostered by the feast would account for its having been the occasion of a certain amount of political disturbance, and for the particular warning about it given to Christians by the Fathers of the Church.[9]

Jerome's statement has the further interest of bringing the feast into relation with the millennium. It is well known that this expression points us to Paradise. A thousand years is the age to which Adam would have lived if he had been faithful, and which his descendants, stricken by original sin, have never been able to reach.[10] So the feast of Tabernacles received a fresh symbolism, which we shall find later in the Fathers; Judaism provides evidence for it too. Its rustic background recalls the original Garden of Eden. Its observances herald the material abundance of the messianic kingdom. Jerusalem restored is Paradise regained. The living water is the river of Paradise flowing in four directions. The *ethrog* carried in procession is a symbol of the fruit of the tree of life (Jerome, *loc. cit.*, 1537A). We know how closely messianic themes are associated with themes of Paradise in Judaism.

That Jerome was testifying to an ancient tradition is proved by the fact that this millenarian understanding of the feast of Tabernacles is already found in Methodius of Olympus. Interpreting the going out from Egypt in an eschatological sense, he writes: "I also, having come out of the Egypt of this life and going on my way, come first to the Resurrection, to the true feast of Tabernacles.

[9] See M. Simon, *Verus Israël* (Paris, 1948), p. 338.
[10] See J. Daniélou, *Théologie du judéo-christianisme* (Paris, 1958), pp. 353–8.

There, having set up my shelter on the first day of the feast, that of judgement, I celebrate the feast with Christ for the thousand years of rest, called the seven days, the true Sabbath. Then I set out for the land of promise, Heaven" (*Conv.*, IX, 5; *G.C.S.*, p. 120). The feast of Tabernacles, then, signifies the earthly rule of the Messiah, before everlasting life. This passage is interesting because it shows that the millenarian idea of the feast was held also by some Christians, as in fact Jerome says it was (1529A). Furthermore, Methodius adhered to Asian theology; and it was in John's Apocalypse and in Papias that there appeared the millenarian as well as the first Christian eschatological symbolism of Tabernacles. The Christians got it from the Jews; and so for them we may date it back to apostolic times.

This is confirmed decisively by Jewish archaeological evidence. One has only to read Erwin Goodenough's work on Jewish symbolism during the Graeco-Roman period[11] to see that the themes most often represented bear on the feast of Tabernacles. This is clear for the *lulab* and the *ethrog*, but the question can also be raised for the *menorah*:[12] Tabernacles was a feast of lights. The *shophar*[13] is associated with the feast of *Rosh-hash-Shanah*, which belongs to the same cycle. The same with the sacrifice of Isaac. Moreover, these symbols are at any rate partly related to the eschatological hope. Whether this hope was messianic or bore on "the beyond" is a question that will have to be touched on in treating of the meanings of these different symbols.

---

[11] *Jewish Symbols in the Graeco-Roman Period*, 11 vols. (New York, 1953–63).

[12] The seven-branched candlestick or lamp-stand.—*Translator.*

[13] A trumpet made from a ram's horn.—*Translator.*

A particularly interesting case is that of the synagogue at Dura-Europos on the Euphrates, where several frescoes have been brought into relation with the feast of Tabernacles. According to du Mesnil du Buisson, one example is fresco W.B.1; but this opinion does not seem tenable.[14] On the other hand, Kraeling thinks that S.B.1, representing the dedication of the Temple, has borrowed features from the feast of Tabernacles: the dedication of the Temple under Solomon in fact took place during the course of that feast. An interesting element is the presence of children, such as is found in Christ's entry into Jerusalem. If this fresco has a messianic significance, as Kraeling thinks (*op. cit.*, p. 117), the feast of Tabernacles, linked to the building of the Temple, would there bear an interpretation of the same order.

But for our purpose the most interesting fresco is the one surrounding the niche of the Torah, and therefore of capital importance. In the middle of the lower part there is a diagrammatic representation of the Temple, with the seven-branched candlestick, the *lulab* and the *ethrog* on its left, and the sacrifice of Isaac on the right. All this refers to the feasts of the month Tishri. The upper part, in its oldest form, shows, according to Kraeling, the tree of life, together with a table and a throne, these symbols having a messianic meaning. One may well ask, then, whether the same is not true of the Temple, the *lulab*, the *ethrog* and the *menorah*. Rachel Wischnitzer does not hesitate to refer this picture to Zacharias 14. 16, and to look on the temple as the eschatological Temple.[15] The over-all conclusion

---

[14] C. H. Kraeling, *The Excavations of Dura-Europos: Final Report*, VIII, 1 (New Haven, Conn., 1956), pp. 118 ff.

[15] *The Messianic Theme in the Paintings of the Dura Synagogue* (Chicago, 1948), p. 89.

of her study is that the only feast unquestionably indicated by those ritual symbols the *lulab* and the *ethrog* is the feast of Tabernacles; but that it is conceived symbolically as a messianic feast, and associated with the central painting of the messianic Temple and the idea of salvation.

This preliminary inquiry shows that Jewish tradition from the days of the prophets to the fourth century after Christ gave a messianic interpretation to the feast of Tabernacles. This is taking the feast as a whole. We must now look at the various elements that make it up. In the first place we shall here find confirmation of what has already been put forward. We shall then be led to disentangle the different eschatological symbolisms with which these elements were clothed in Judaic Christianity during the period under consideration. Finally we shall look at the Jewish literary and archaeological evidence, and also at Judaeo-Christian data which seem simply to echo an earlier symbolism.

First of all there are the leafy arbours, the σκηναί, the "tabernacles". This is doubtless one of the elements with the oldest messianic significance. There is perhaps an allusion to them in Isaias 32. 18, where the life of the righteous in the messianic kingdom is represented as a dwelling in arbours of peace. Starting from this theme, a messianic significance came to be given to the arbours of the feast of Tabernacles, as Harald Riesenfeld sees: "The arbours were thought of not only as a memory of divine protection in the wilderness, but also—and this is important—as prefiguring the *sukkoth* in which the righteous will dwell in the world to come. So it appears that a very precise eschatological significance was given to the most characteristic observance of the feast of Tabernacles, as it was celebrated in Judaic times."[16]

Doubtless the New Testament "everlasting dwellings" (αἰώνιοι σκηναί) mentioned in Luke 16. 9 must be explained in the same context. In the Apocalypse the expressions σκηναί and the corresponding verb σκηνῶ are used several times to designate the habitation of the righteous in Heaven (7. 15; 12. 12; 13. 6; 21. 3); and we shall see that the Apocalypse is full of references to the feast of Tabernacles. But above all it seems very likely that we may, with Riesenfeld, regard the eschatological symbolism of the arbours as the key to a most important New Testament happening, namely, the Transfiguration. Several of its aspects agree in suggesting a relationship between it and the feast of Tabernacles. The first is chronological. Mark (9. 2 [1]) and Matthew (17. 1) say that the Transfiguration happened "six days afterwards", while Luke (9. 28) says "about eight days after". The difference suggests that it was an occasion of the year when the interval of six to eight days had a special relevance. Now this was particularly true of the feast of Tabernacles, which lasted eight days, the eighth being of special importance.

A second point is geographical, that of the mountain. We have remarked the particular link between the feast and the Mount of Olives. In Zacharias, the glory of Yahweh was to appear on the Mount of Olives: and Christ manifests himself in glory on a mountain, unidentified. The cloud (Luke 9. 34) has a tie with the worship in the Temple: here it is the expression of Yahweh's dwelling

---

[16] *Jésus transfiguré* (Copenhagen, 1947), pp. 188–9. See J. Bonsirven, *Le Judaisme palestinien au temps de Jésus-Christ*, 1 (Paris, 1945), p. 522; H. Sahlin, *Zur Typologie des Johannesevangeliums* (Uppsala, 1950), p. 54.

amid the just in the world to come. Riesenfeld also points out that the words "It is good for us to be here" (Luke 9. 33) could be the expression of the state of rest, the eschatological ἀνάπαυσις, whose connection with living in tabernacles we have just seen in Isaias 32. 18.[17]

This throws light on another and most mysterious matter: Peter's proposal to make arbours (σηκναί) for the Messiah, for Moses and for Elias. It certainly looks as if we must see in these arbours an allusion to the feast of Tabernacles. Peter would be taking the manifestation of Jesus' glory as a sign that the messianic times were come. But one of the characteristics of those times was to be the righteous living in arbours, which were prefigured by the arbours of the feast of Tabernacles. From this point of view Peter's suggestion becomes clearly explicable: it expresses his faith in the effective fulfilment of the messianic times under the form of the observances of the feast of Tabernacles.[18] The incident is still more intelligible if it took place at the time when Tabernacles was being celebrated. We shall come back to this.

There is a last observation to be made about the eschatological significance of the arbours, concerning their symbolism. Methodius sees them as a symbol of our risen bodies during the millennium (*Conv.*, IX, 2; *G.C.S.*, p. 116). Bodies are likened to "tabernacles" in Wisdom 9. 15; 2 Cor. 5. 1, 4 and 2 Peter 1. 13; but the reference of these texts to the feast of Tabernacles is debated, and the point will be referred to again later. One of the oldest biblical texts used by Christians in associating the idea of resurrection with that of a tabernacle raised up is Amos 9. 11: "I will raise up (ἀναστήσω) the tabernacle of

---

[17] Riesenfeld, *op. cit.*, pp. 258–61.
[18] B. Zielenski, "De sensu Transfigurationis", in *V.D.*, 26 (1948), p. 342.

David." This text is included among the *testimonia* used by Irenaeus (*Dem.*, 38 and 62; *P.O.*, 12, pp. 688 and 707) as foretelling Christ's resurrection; and it had already occurred in the *testimonia* of Qumran, but without any reference to resurrection (*C.D.C.*, VII, 14–19). So it does not seem that the associating of the arbours of the feast with risen bodies antedates Christianity.

But we do find in Judaism another symbolism, concerning not the arbours themselves but their decoration. Riesenfeld points out that the *midrashim* are familiar with the idea that the adornment of the dwellings of the future will accord with a man's actions during his earthly life.[19] This is going in the direction of a symbolism that we shall find in the *lulab* and the *ethrog*. The interesting point for us is that the symbolism of the dwellings' adornment is found also in Christian tradition, which here surely depends on a rabbinic symbolism. Methodius writes: During the millennium "I celebrate a feast to God according to the Law, adorning my bodily tabernacle [i.e., the risen body] with good deeds. If I can display fruits of virtue when I come to be examined on the first day of resurrection, then I shall be bearing what is expected of me. If the *Skenopegia* is the resurrection, then the things prescribed for the adornment of the arbours are the works of holiness" (*Conv.*, IX, 17; *G.C.S.*, p. 116, ll. 20–7). And St Ephraem writes: In Paradise "I saw the tents (σκηναί) of the righteous made fresh with sweet scents, decked with fruit, garlanded with flowers. The greater a man's struggle to obtain virtue, the more lovely will be his tabernacle" (*Hymn. Parad.*, V, 6; E. Beck, *Studia Anselmiana*, 26, p. 41). Beck expressly notes that the tents have a relation to the feast of Tabernacles.

[19] Riesenfeld, *op. cit.*, p. 197.

This brings us to a second series of symbols, the *lulab* and the *ethrog*, whose eschatological and messianic significance in the Judaism of Christ's day is certain. They are the objects most often represented on Jewish monuments, and Goodenough has devoted a long study to them (IV, pp. 145–66). In the first place one notices their association with the messianic hope. Riesenfeld has drawn attention to a passage in the *Testament of Nephtali* (V, 4): Nephtali has a vision on the Mount of Olives, in which Levi, having vanquished the sun, himself becomes as shining as the sun. He is then given twelve palms. When we reflect on the connections of the feast of Tabernacles and the Mount of Olives with the messianic expectation, we can but see here an appearing of the Messiah, like the rising sun, on the Mount of Olives during the feast of Tabernacles. Accordingly, the palms are the token of his victory.[20] How can we fail to associate the episode with the appearing of Christ on the Mount of Olives at the time of his triumphal entry into Jerusalem? The *lulab* and *ethrog* in the central panel at the Dura-Europos synagogue can be interpreted in the same messianic sense.

But side by side with this messianic meaning there is one much more important, concerning the eschatological hope in the after life. It is this that accounts for the very frequent presence of the *lulab* and the *ethrog* on Jewish funerary monuments, of which Goodenough supplies many examples. Here the symbolism is not of victory but of resurrection.[21] It is noteworthy that the palm is found on a Judaeo-Christian stele in Palestine, of which Father E. Testa has sent me a photograph. This is the context that gives its meaning to the palms carried by martyrs,

[20] See Strack-Billerbeck, II, pp. 789–90.
[21] Riesenfeld, *op. cit.*, pp. 34–6.

men who have overcome death; the idea is found already in the Apocalypse (7. 9). It will be noticed that both in the *Testament of Nephtali* and on the monuments it is a matter simply of palms, and not of the *lulab* properly so called. But Goodenough thinks that the *lulab* was none the less intended, for the palm was its most characteristic and representative part and came to stand for the whole. And it represents here the hope of immortality.[22]

There is another symbolism of the *lulab* to be noticed, which ties up with what has been said about the branches adorning the arbours; it indicates the good works which have their reward at the last day. This appears in the extension of one of the observances of the Tabernacles feast: on the first day the Jews had to submit the *lulab* for examination to ensure that its component sprigs were in good condition.[23] A passage in the *Shepherd* of Hermas, a document of Judaeo-Christian character, seems to supply the symbolism of this rite; it is a passage whose connection with the feast of Tabernacles is quite evident to me. It shows a glorious angel of the Lord distributing branches of willow to the crowd, and then asking them back from each person. To each of those whose branches are in bud he gives a crown. Those whose branches are dry and withered he sends away. The angel then explains that the branches are the Law; those whose branches are dry are those who have been neglectful of it (*Sim.*, VIII, 2, 1–4). This shows clearly that this symbolism had persisted among Christians.

So far reference has been made only to the *lulab*. The *ethrog* shares its eschatological symbolism. It is often found with the *lulab* on funerary monuments, and with the

[22] See Goodenough, *op. cit.*, p. 165.
[23] See Strack-Billerbeck, II, pp. 792–93.

same significance of immortality. The Fathers of the
Church were to see in the *ethrog* a symbol of the fruit of
the tree of life in Paradise. Several Jewish or Judaeo-
Christian texts look on the fruit of the tree of life as an
expression of eternal life.[24] Was there already in Judaism
a connection between this symbolism and that of the
ethrog?[25] Here it is interesting to compare Ezechiel 47. 12
with Zacharias 14. 16. The two chapters clearly depend
on one another; there is the living water that will flow out
from the new Jerusalem through the Mount of Olives
(Ez. 47. 8; Zach. 14. 4, 8). Ezechiel shows us growing on
the banks of this torrent trees that bring forth fruit each
month. This is the idea which is taken up by the Apocalypse, in 22. 2. To that there corresponds the feast of
Tabernacles in Zacharias (14. 16). In either case there is
question of the Mount of Olives, whose connection with
the feast of Tabernacles has already been mentioned. We
may, then, conclude that the feast was regarded as a
figure of Paradise, and that the *ethrog* here corresponded to
the fruit of the tree of life.

One last theme calls for separate treatment, because it is
generally ignored when the feast of Tabernacles and its
messianic symbolism are being examined, namely, the
crown. There is an opinion current that the use of a crown
is foreign to Judaism, and that when it occurs it is a pagan
infiltration. This is the argument of Büchler, Baus,
Goodenough and Baron in particular.[26] As for Christians,
appeal is made to Tertullian's *De corona militum*, which

---

[24] *1 Enoch*, 25. 4–5; *Test. Lev.*, 18. 11; *Apoc.* 2. 7; 22. 2.
[25] See Riesenfeld, *op. cit*, pp. 34–6.
[26] See the references in my "Bulletin des Origines chrétiennes", in
R.S.R., 45 (1957), p. 612.

condemns the use of crowns. On the other hand, a number of writers have opposed this view. Harald Riesenfeld,[27] Jacques Dupont[28] and Isaac Abrahams[29] defend the Jewish origin of the crown, and this opinion seems to us to be well-founded. But it also seems that one can go further and connect the use of crowns, first by the Jews and then by the Christians, with the feast of Tabernacles. And this enables us to have a better understanding of its eschatological symbolism.

The wearing of crowns in the procession round the altar on the eighth day of the feast is attested by both Jewish and pagan sources. The essential Jewish text is the *Book of Jubilees*, 16. 30: "It is ordained for ever regarding Israel that they should celebrate it [the feast of Tabernacles] and dwell in arbours, and set wreaths on their heads and carry leafy boughs and branches of willow." The crowns mentioned are obviously chaplets of leaves. This piece of information is confirmed by the description of the feast given by Tacitus (*Hist.*, v, 5), in which he states that the Jewish priests then wore crowns of ivy. Goodenough writes that it is reasonable to suppose that these two wholly independent sources establish the fact, ignored by the rabbis in the Talmud, that the Hellenistic custom of wearing crowns had been introduced among the customs of the Jewish feast.[30] The agreement of the texts indeed establishes the existence of the custom. But there is no justification for the statement that it is Hellenistic in origin. The allusion in the *Book of Jubilees* establishes the contrary.

To these texts may be added a Christian one, but having

[27] *Jésus transfiguré*, pp. 48–51.
[28] *Σὺν Χριστῷ: L'union avec le Christ suivant saint Paul* (Louvain, 1952), p. 78.
[29] *Studies in Pharisaism and the Gospels* (Cambridge, 1917), I, pp. 169–70.
[30] *Jewish Symbols*, IV, p. 157.

the Jewish feast as its context, from Parable VIII of Hermas. We have mentioned this passage above, because of its reference to the *lulab* as symbolical of good works. It describes a vision of the Judgement within the framework of the feast of Tabernacles. And in it we read: "The angel of the Lord called for crowns, and they were brought, seemingly made from palm leaves. And he crowned the men who had given up their branches bearing buds and fruit" (*Sim.*, VIII, 2, 1). Notice that these crowns are said to be made of palm. Origen mentions a Judaeo-Christian book in which "all the believers receive a crown of willow" (*Hom. Ezech.*, 1, 5), and it has been suggested that this book was *The Shepherd*; but the different material of the crown seems to contradict the identification. This reference also could be to the feast of Tabernacles, for sprigs of willow formed part of the *lulab*, and so could be used for the crowns too.

Jewish pictorial monuments confirm these literary documents. A fresco in the synagogue at Dura-Europos, which, all agree, represents the Tabernacles procession, depicts priests wearing crowns of flowers.[31] An inscription at Berenike in Cyrenaica, dated a little before Christ, shows the local Jews presenting a crown of olive to a magistrate during the feast of Tabernacles.[32] But the main fact, brought out by Goodenough, is the frequent association of the crown with the *lulab* on Jewish funerary monuments.[33] All the evidence associates the *lulab* with the feast of Tabernacles, and so it is very likely that it was the same for the crown.[34]

---

[31] See Kraeling, *op. cit.*, pp. 114–15.
[32] Goodenough, *op. cit.*, II, pp. 143–4.
[33] *Ibid.*, III, pl. 471; IV, p. 157.
[34] Goodenough gives further evidence, *op. cit.*, VII, pp. 151–2.

Final confirmation comes from Judaeo-Christian texts concerning baptism. Crowns are often mentioned in the *Odes of Solomon*. Thus, at the beginning of Ode I: "The Lord is on my head like a crown, and I shall not be without him. A crown of truth has been woven for me." Ode xx, 7–8 makes it clear that a crown of foliage is meant: "Come into his Paradise, and make thee a garland from its tree and put it on thy head." J. H. Bernard believes that these passages allude to a liturgical custom, and refers to the baptismal rite, wherein the neophyte is crowned with flowers.[35] G. W. H. Lampe accepts this hypothesis; for the author of the *Odes*, he writes, "the neophyte is apparently crowned with a garland, symbolizing the presence of Christ, like a crown on the head of the believer".[36] This usage here surely derives from Judaism, wherein the context of the crown is the feast of Tabernacles. When, furthermore, we recall that the Judaeo-Christian rites of baptism contain other allusions to that feast,[37] it is readily believable that the Syro-Christian use of the crown originated in the Jewish rites of Tabernacles.

The *Testament of Levi* furnishes evidence that is more precise still, and all the more valuable in that the Jewish elements are very apparent beneath the Christian writing. The relevant passage is one in which T. W. Manson and M. de Jonge see an evocation of Christian baptism under the symbol of the enthronement of the high-priest. Seven men conduct this initiation. The first makes an anointing with oil and delivers a staff; the second gives a washing in pure water, presents bread and wine, and

---

[35] *The Odes of Solomon* (Cambridge, 1912), p. 45.
[36] *The Seal of the Spirit* (London, 1951), p. 112. See J. Daniélou, *Théologie du judéo-christianisme*, p. 382.
[37] J. Daniélou, *Les Quatre-Temps . . .*, pp. 114–16.

confers a robe of honour. The fifth gives a branch of olive. The sixth puts a crown on the head (8, 4–9). The association of an olive branch and a crown sets the context of the feast of Tabernacles, and is evidence for the connection of crowns with it; but the rites taken as a whole seem to be referred to baptism. So the crown appears here as a Christian baptismal observance derived from Jewish customs at the feast of Tabernacles.

Finally, the *Book of Jeû* provides a gnostic baptismal ritual with several mentions of crowning, which the context shows to be suggested by Jewish customs. The most important passage says that "Jesus carried out this mystery (μυστήριον), while all his disciples were robed in linen garments and crowned with a crown of myrtle" (47; *G.C.S.*, p. 312). So we have the combination of a white garment and a crown, as in the *Testament of Levi*. But the crown is of myrtle. As we know, myrtle was the third component of the *lulab*, with palm and willow, and we have already met these two in crowns, which it seems could be of several different kinds. There are references to crowns of ivy and of roses; and the *Book of Jeû* mentions in the baptismal ritual others of verbena (περιστερεὼν ὀρθός) and of wormwood (ἀρτεμισία).[38]

So the use of crowns of foliage in the rites of the feast of Tabernacles is attested both by Jewish documents about the feast and by Judaeo-Christian documents which show it persisting in the rites of baptism.[39] This enables us to arrive at one last aspect of the Jewish symbolism of the feast. The eschatological character of the crown

[38] 46; *G.C.S.*, p. 309; 48; *G.C.S.*, p. 313.—The rite of crowning has an important place in the Mandaean baptismal ritual. See E. Segelberg, *Masbûtâ: Studies in the Ritual of the Mandaean Baptism* (Uppsala, 1958), p. 61. But there is nothing Hellenistic about Mandaean usages.

[39] See also Cyril of Jerusalem, *Procatech.*, 1; *P.G.*, 33, 332A.

as denoting eternal blessedness is clear. We will give some examples. But this symbol is often associated with the Hellenistic practice of giving a crown to a victor, as is done by Christian writers, for instance, in 1 Cor. 9. 25. However, there is a whole series of Jewish and Christian texts in which the crown is the symbol of the glory of the elect, in the biblical sense of the word, and of the imperishable life which is their lot. And this symbolism is connected with the use of the crown during the feast of Tabernacles and with the eschatological meaning of that feast.

For the Jews, this is proved by the figured monuments: the crown is a symbol of the hope of immortality. It is associated in this symbolism with the *lulab*, whose connection with the feast of Tabernacles is obvious. We have quoted Goodenough on this matter. For the Christians, we have pointed out the eschatological symbolism of the crown in *The Shepherd*, in a context which is that of the eschatological feast of Tabernacles. But there are other examples. The Apocalypse of St John (2. 10) shows us "the crown of life" given to him who is "faithful unto death". Just before this (2. 7), fruit from "the tree of life" has a parallel symbolism, and we have seen the connection of this with the *ethrog*. The "palm branches in their hands" (7. 9) are another symbol of the glory of the elect; everything goes to show that they refer to the *lulab*. As J. Comblin has demonstrated, the Apocalypse is shot through with imagery from the feast of Tabernacles.[40] For John, the procession of white-robed priests on the eighth day of the feast becomes the symbol of the procession of the elect round the altar in Heaven on the eighth day which follows the cosmic week. The crown of life is an element in the same transposition.

[40] "La Liturgie de la Nouvelle Jerusalem", in *E.T.L.*, 29 (1953), pp. 27–40.

This again is found elsewhere in Christian apocalyptic writings. For the *Ascension of Isaias* the crown, together with the garment, is the symbol of the glory of the elect; clothing and crown are kept in readiness at the seventh heaven, to be put on by Isaias when he enters there (7. 22; see also 8. 26; 9. 25). It will be noticed that the crown represents the supreme glory and follows the garment, which may be a reference to a ritual order. The *Apocalypse of Peter* also mentions the crowns in an eschatological context (*R.O.C.*, 5 [1910], pp. 317–19). The *Testament of Benjamin* speaks of "crowns of glory worn by those who have shown mercy" (4. 1). The eschatological significance of crowns is expressed in various ways. The "crown of life" in Apocalypse 2. 10 appears again in James 1. 12: the man "who endures under trials . . . will win the crown of life". 1 Peter 5. 4 speaks of the "crown of glory" in a passage which recalls Apocalypse 7. 17: "When the prince of shepherds shall appear, you shall receive a never-fading crown of glory."

There is a last text, in 5 [2] *Esdras*, which brings together the crown and other eschatological themes that we have mentioned. In its description of the eschatological promises we find the "everlasting dwellings" and the "tree of life" (2. 11–12). There is the theme of twelve trees, associated with springs flowing with milk and honey, and with seven mountains (2. 18–19), putting us in the context of Ezechiel 47 and Apocalypse 22. The elect are dressed in white (2. 39–40). But the crucial passage is this: "In their midst was a young man of great stature, taller than any of the others, and on the head of each of them he placed a crown, and each then became taller. . . . Then I asked an angel, 'Who are these, my lord?' He answered, 'These are they who have put off mortal clothing and put on the immortal, and they have confessed the name of God; now they are being crowned and receive palms – *modo coronantur et accipiunt palmas'*. Then I said to the angel, 'Who is that young man who places crowns on them and puts palms in their hands?' He answered and said to me, 'He is the Son of God, whom they confessed in the world'" (2. 43–7).[41]

Notice first the features which relate this text to *The Shepherd*. The Son of God is distinguished by his great height (*Sim.*, VIII, I, 2). The name of God is a synonym for the Son of God (*Sim.*, VIII, 6, 2).[42] Twelve mountains are described in Parable IX, I, 4 ff. The tall young man distributing crowns and palms agrees with Parable VIII, 2, I, where the context is the feast of Tabernacles; it is natural to conclude that it is the same in *5 Esdras*. Then there is the reference to white garments, which is found also in Parable VIII, 2, 3. These analogies give an answer to the disputed question of the date of this apocryphal work, *5 Esdras*. The inclination has been to assign it to the fifth century, because its influence on Christian art and liturgy becomes noticeable at that time.[43] But the analogies with *The Shepherd* enable H. Weinel and G. Volkmar to put it at the end of the second century and to associate it with Judaeo-Christian literature. Like *The Shepherd*, it may have been translated in the fourth century.[44]

The very special interest of this document is that through it a number of Judaeo-Christian eschatological themes from the feast of Tabernacles passed into the Roman

[41] See J. Labourt, "Le Cinquième Livre d'Esdras", in *R.B.*, 6 (1909), pp. 433–4; the textual variants are given.
[42] See J. Daniélou, *Théologie du judéo-christianisme*, pp. 204–8.
[43] See L. Pirot, "Le Cinquième Livre d'Esdras", in *S.D.B.*, II, cc. 1103–7.
[44] "Das Fünfte Buch Esra", in Hennecke, *Neutestamentliche Apokryphen*, pp. 390–1.

liturgy and Roman art. We owe to it, for instance, the verse *Requiem aeternam* in the Mass for the dead; we have seen that "rest" was one theme of the feast. But here we are interested in the crowns. The verse *Modo coronantur et accipiunt palmas* was introduced into the second nocturn of the common office of the apostles;[45] and a mosaic in the church of St Praxedes in Rome depicts the elect clothed in white robes and carrying palms and crowns. This is unknown to previous Christian art, and it seems that it can be explained only by the diffusion of this apocryphal writing in fourth-century Rome. Through it the crowns of the feast of Tabernacles found their way to the Christian West.

But if the eschatological symbolism of the crown was late in appearing in the West, it seems to have always existed in the East, and to have been used in the liturgy. There is evidence of this in St Ephraem's *Hymns on Paradise*. We have already remarked that his picture of Paradise drew its inspiration from the feast of Tabernacles, and this is true of the "tabernacles" themselves, with their decoration and symbolism. He often mentions crowns also. In Hymn VI we see the just arriving in Paradise with boughs bearing the flowers and fruit of their merits, which they plait into crowns for themselves (12, 15; Beck, pp. 53–4). This use of flowering branches presents a quite different image from that of the palm awarded to the victor in the races of the Greek world.[46]

---

[45] See L. Brou, "Le Quatrième Livre d'Esdras dans la liturgie hispanique", in *Sacris Erudiri*, 9 (1957), pp. 74–9.

[46] In *The Epistle of James and Judaic Christianity* (Cambridge, 1927), p. 40, G. H. Rendall emphasizes the Jewish origin of the expression; he points out that the crown is the equivalent of the Hebrew *atarah* and has no connection with the victor's crown at the games, which is foreign to St James's background.

It is the foremost image that we meet in Hermas, in Methodius of Olympus, in Ephraem—and rabbinic tradition testifies to it.

It is possible that the crown had other uses in Judaism; it is found mentioned in other contexts, as in Judith 15. 13 (according to the Septuagint). There are also allusions to diadems and their symbolism in the Bible; but we are here confining ourselves to the use of crowns of foliage at the feast of Tabernacles. And in view of the evidence as a whole, it does seem that it is with this use that we must connect the Jewish and Judaeo-Christian symbolism of the crown as a sign of eschatological glory. This usage, and its symbolism, makes a relatively late appearance in Judaism: it is found in connection with the development of messianic expectancy and with apocalyptic writings in literature. But it shows no dependence on Hellenism. Later on, its symbolism is mingled with the Greek symbolism of the crown as the victor's prize at the games, as we see in St Paul. This evolution is parallel with that of the eschatological glory, when the biblical *kabod* became tinged with the content of the Greek δόξα and the Roman *gloria*.[47] But the original biblical connotation nevertheless persisted.

We can now follow the history and exegesis of the feast of Tabernacles and appreciate its importance for the beginnings of Christian liturgy and eschatology. Judaism gave it an eschatological interpretation, bearing on its significance as a whole. Further, several Jewish specifically eschatological symbols—the *lulab*, the *ethrog*, the

[47] See J. Daniélou, "Bulletin d'histoire des origines chrétiennes", in *R.S.R.*, 45 (1957), pp. 611–13.

crown—can be connected with it. These symbols continued to live in Christian liturgy. They are given a large place in pictorial monuments. They become the inspiration of eschatological symbolism. Here we have a particular aspect of the typology of Jewish feasts in Christianity that can be added to that of Easter and of Pentecost.

2

The Vine and the Tree of Life

A remarkable feature of Judaeo-Christian literature is the place held in it by the Church. Elsewhere I have studied some of the themes used to delineate the mystery of her grandeur. She is the aged woman, older than the world, who appears to Hermas; she is the tower which he sees angels building; she is the bride of the Word, whom Clement of Rome shows us. Another theme occurring many times is that of the Church as "plantation" (φυτεία), a theme whose Judaeo-Christian character can now be confirmed by parallels in the Qumran manuscripts. It has variants, too, which add further elements to primitive Christianity's *mystique* of the Church.

First we will set out the Judaeo-Christian texts that are directly connected with our theme; the fact that H. Schlier has brought them together enables us to do so more easily.[1] In the *Ascension of Isaias* there is mention of "the plantation planted by the twelve apostles of the Well-Beloved" (4, 3).[2] Ignatius of Antioch twice uses the word φυτεία: "Keep away from the weeds (βοτανῶν), which Jesus Christ does not tend, for they are not of the Father's planting (φυτεία)"(*Philad.*, III, 1); "Shun the evil offshoots, whose fruit is deadly; . . . they are not of the Father's planting (φυτεία)" (*Trall.*, XI,   1. See also VI,

[1] *Religionsgeschichtliche Untersuchungen zu den Ignatiusbriefen* (Giessen, 1929), pp. 48–54.

[2] See 1 Cor. 3. 6: "I have planted (ἐφύτευσα), Apollo watered : but God gave the increase."

1 and *Eph.*, x, 3 for "weeds"). These texts recall Matthew 15. 13: "Every plant (φυτεία) which my heavenly Father hath not planted shall be rooted up."[3]

The *Odes of Solomon* provide more developed examples: "Blessed, O Lord, are they who are planted in thy land! for whom there is a place in your Paradise. When they were planted in your earth . . . they turned back the bitterness of the trees from them" (xi, 15, 18). And in xxxviii, 17–21: "My foundations were laid on the hand of the Lord: because he established me. For he set the root and watered it and fixed it and blessed it; and its fruits are for ever. . . . The Lord alone was glorified in his planting and in his husbandry . . . by the beautiful planting of his right hand: and by the splendour of his planting." The first of these passages is particularly interesting. The place of the plantation is Paradise; each plant represents a baptized person; the gardener is the Lord. Notice, too, the opposition between the plants of Paradise and the bitter trees that are outside.

There is a passage reminiscent of the *Odes of Solomon* in the *Gospel of Truth* found at Nag-Hammadi: "He knows his own plants, because it is he who planted them in his Paradise" (xxxvi, 35–8). It is the theme of the plantation again. This work is possibly a homily for baptism or confirmation; in any case the baptismal and catechetical connotation is striking. There are the same images as in the *Odes*: the plantation which corresponds to baptism; the plants are those who are baptized; Paradise is the Church; God is the gardener. Here indeed is a theme of Judaeo-Christian catechesis, inherited from Jewish

---

[3] H. Riesenfeld connects the theme in Matthew and St Paul with Ezechiel 17. 1–8 (*Le langage parabolique chez Paul* . . . [Desclée, 1960], pp. 54–5). But in Ezechiel there is mention of only one single vine.

catechesis and to be found in both orthodox and hetero-
dox Judaic Christianity.[4]

These texts all have one and the same underlying
symbolism. The plantation denotes a collective thing; it
is planted by God; its plants are many and various; it
fills Paradise. This plantation represents the Church,
formed of many plants. Each one of them is an individual,
and his being planted in Paradise corresponds to baptism;
it makes him a member of the Church. The plantation is
in varying degrees the work of the Father, of our Lord,
of the apostles. To the Father's plantation are opposed the
weeds, which he has not planted. Ignatius of Antioch
identifies the weeds with heresies. The atmosphere is
plainly ecclesiological and baptismal.

This theme of the Church as "God's plantation" is
carried on. The *Teaching of the Apostles* (third century), in
the Greek version in Book I of the *Apostolic Constitutions*,
begins with these words: "The catholic Church is God's
plantation ($\phi v \tau \epsilon i \alpha$) and those who believe his true revela-
tion are the chosen vineyard ($\dot{\alpha} \mu \pi \epsilon \lambda \dot{\omega} v$)" (*Praef.*; Funk,
p. 3). Later on we shall meet the vineyard theme which
derives from Isaias 5. 1. The image called up by $\phi v \tau \epsilon i \alpha$,
that of a plant put in the ground, appears in Clement of
Alexandria (*Strom.*, VI, 1, 2, 4): "Our gnosis and spiritual
paradise is the Saviour himself: we are planted ($\kappa \alpha \tau \alpha$-
$\phi v \tau \epsilon v \dot{o} \mu \epsilon \theta \alpha$) in him, being transferred and transplanted
($\mu \epsilon \tau \alpha \mu o \sigma \chi \epsilon v \theta \dot{\epsilon} v \tau \epsilon s$) from the old life into good soil. And
with this change of plantation ($\phi v \tau \epsilon i \alpha$) comes the growth of
much fruit ($\epsilon \dot{v} \kappa \alpha \rho \pi i \alpha$)."

Now this imagery clearly reflects Judaism in the time of

[4] See E. Segelberg, "Evangelium Veritatis: A Confirmation Homily
and its Relation to the Odes of Solomon", in *Orientalia Suecana*, 8 (1959),
pp. 1-42.

Christ, and it certainly has its roots in the Old Testament. We read in Isaias: "They [the remnant of Israel] shall be called the planting (φύτευμα) of the Lord to glorify him" (61. 3; see 60. 21).[5] But it had a remarkable development in Jewish apocalyptic writings. In *1 Enoch* there occurs the expression "plant of justice and truth", designating the chosen people (10. 16; see also 62. 8; 84. 6; 93. 2). This may be a reference to the idea of one unique plant, which will be mentioned later. The *Psalms of Solomon* provide a closer expression: "The Lord's paradise, the trees of life, are his saints. Their planting (φυτεία) is rooted for eternity; they shall not be plucked out so long as heaven lasts" (XIV, 3–4).[6]

But it is the Qumran manuscripts which here give the most valuable documentation. The expression keeps on occurring. The Council of the Community "will be made steadfast in truth in as much as it is the eternal plantation" (*D.S.D.*, VIII, 5). Bertil Gärtner writes with reference to this text: "In the *Manual of Discipline* we find the word 'plantation' used as a technical term for the sect, which considers itself to be the holy remnant."[7] The expression is found also in *D.S.D.*, XI, 8, and in *C.D.C.*, I, 7. Above all, it finds a considerable place in the *Hodayoth*, the implied allusions being particularly abundant. The "eternal plantation" stands for the community: "All the rivers of Eden water it" (VI, 15–17). The whole of column 8 is devoted to the theme.[8] The plantation is made up of living trees (VIII, 5). These

---

[5] On this text see I. F. M. Brawley, "Yahweh is the Guardian of his Plantation: a Note on Is., 60. 21", in *Biblica*, 41 (1960), pp. 275–87.

[6] See H. Riesenfeld, *Jésus transfiguré*, pp. 190 ff.; Philo, *Opif.*, 153: "All the trees in God's paradise are alive and rational."

[7] *Die rätselhaften Termini Nazoräer und Iskariot* (Uppsala, 1957), p. 23.

[8] See G. Bernini, "Il Giardiniere della Piantagione Eterna (D.S.T., VIII)", in *Sacra Pagina* (Bibl. E.T.L., 63. Louvain, 1959), II, pp. 47–59.

trees do not cease to bear fruit for ever (VIII, 20). The trees of life are the blessed, and to them are opposed the trees of water (VIII, 9). The planting of the trees is described at length (VIII, 21–6). Here there are striking resemblances to the *Odes of Solomon*: they have been pointed out by A. Dupont-Sommer.[9] In a final passage, the holy are again likened to living trees (x, 26).

Mandaeism furnishes a last important testimony to the plantation image in pre-Christian Judaism. Mandaeism is a Jewish gnosis,[10] and Schlier (*op. cit.*, pp. 48–61) and Gärtner (*op. cit.*, pp. 25–33) have shown the importance of the plantation theme in it. The first-named in particular has brought out the closeness between Mandaean and Judaeo-Christian texts: "I have come into the world", says the Gardener, "to plant the plantation of life" *Das Johannesbuch der Mandäer*, Lidzbarski); and: "How fine are the plants which the Jordan has planted and reared. They have borne perfect fruit" (*Mandäische Liturgien*, Lidzbarski). The link between the plantation and the Jordan must be noticed: it recalls that between the plantation and the rivers of Eden in the *Hodayoth*. The theme's baptismal character is again manifest here; and it must be added that the Mandaean liturgy of baptism includes the planting of a branch of willow in the Jordan.[11]

We may, then, consider as established the connection of the theme of the plantation representing the Church with Judaeo-Christian baptismal catechesis; this latter

[9] *The Essene Writings from Qumrân* (Oxford, 1961). See also F.-M. Braun, *Jean le Théologien et son Évangile dans l'Église ancienne* (Paris, 1959), pp. 228–9.

[10] See K. Rudolph, *Die Mandäer, I: Das Mandäerproblem* (Göttingen, 1960), p. 252, the most recent work.

[11] Segelberg, *Masbûtâ*, pp. 41–5.

was, in turn, affected by Jewish catechesis. In later Christianity it came to be combined with other elements, and in the first place with the garden, the paradise which we have already met. The Church is God's paradise, its trees are individual Christians, planted therein by baptism. We read in Irenaeus: "Men who have advanced in faith and received God's Spirit are spiritual, planted as it were in Paradise" (*Adv. haer.*, v, 10, 1). Already in the New Testament baptism is thought of as a planting, for Paul calls the newly baptized "neophytes", the newly planted (1 Tim. 3. 6). Later writings prefer another, more Greek, image, the "newly enlightened (νεοφώτιστοι)".[12]

Hippolytus of Rome expands the theme quite plainly: "Eden is the name of the new garden of delights, planted towards the East, furnished with every good tree, by which must be understood the company of the just. . . . The harmony of all, the saints' way to fellowship, is the Church, God's spiritual garden, planted in Christ as in the East: here may be seen every sort of tree, the line of patriarchs . . . and prophets . . . , the choir of apostles . . . , the procession of virgins . . . , the order of bishops, priests and levites. . . . An inexhaustible river flows through this garden, and from it four streams water the whole earth. So it is with the Church. Christ is the river, and he is proclaimed to the world by the four gospels" (*Com. Dan.*, 1, 17; *G.C.S.*, p. 28, ll. 16 ff.). This is right in the line of the *Hodayoth* and the Mandaean writings. The garden is the Church, its trees are the holy ones, and it is watered by the river of living water, which is Christ.[13]

---

[12] See J. Daniélou, "Catéchèse pascale et retour au Paradis", in *La Maison-Dieu*, 45 (1956), p. 101.

[13] On this theme in archaeology, see P. A. Underwood, "The Fountain of Life", in *Dumbarton Oaks Papers*, 51 (1950), pp. 43–138.

The theme of various trees corresponding to the various orders in the Church is found again in Optatus of Milevis (*Schism. Donat.*, II, 11). St Cyprian comes close to Hippolytus when he writes: "The Church, like Paradise, includes fruit-bearing trees within her walls. . . . She waters the trees from four rivers, which are the four gospels, by which she dispenses the grace of baptism" (*Epist.*, 73, 10). The four streams underline the paradisial nature of the plantation; the *Hodayoth* had already shown it to be watered by "all the rivers of Eden". The theme's catechetical character is shown from its use everywhere. Thus, in Origen: "Those who are born again in baptism are placed in Paradise, that is, in the Church, there to carry out inward spiritual works" (*Com. Gen.* 2. 16; *P. G.*, 12, 100 BC). And in Ephraem: "God has planted a beautiful garden. He has built up his spotless Church. In the midst of the Church he has planted the Word. The company of the holy ones is like Paradise" (*Hymn. Parad.*, VI, 7-9).

Ephraem's words include a point that we have not yet taken up. The Word is the tree of life planted in the middle of Paradise. Hippolytus compares the Word to the water of Paradise, but also to the tree of life: "In this Paradise were found the tree of knowledge and the tree of life. In the same way today, there are two trees planted in Paradise, the Law and the Word" (*Com. Dan.*, I, 17; *G.C.S.*, p. 29, ll. 16-19). This is also found in a document we have not previously quoted, whose thought is close to that of Hippolytus, the *Epistle to Diognetus*: "Those who really love God become a paradise of delights, causing to grow within them a fruitful, flourishing (εὐθαλοῦν) tree; they are adorned with fine fruits. For this is the ground in which have been planted the tree of knowledge and the tree of life . . . showing that life is attained through knowledge" (12, 1–3). Here again it would seem that the image is that of Paradise as a fellowship of the holy: each one of them is a fruit-bearing tree; and at the centre of this Paradise the Word bestows knowledge and life: "Let the Word of truth, received within yourself, become your life" (XII, 7).

The topic of Christ as tree of life recurs frequently: for example, in Justin, *Dialogue with Trypho*, LXXXVI, 1; Clement of Alexandria, *Stromata*, III, 17, 103, 4 and V, 11, 72, 2;[14] Origen, *Com. Joh.*, XX, 36; *G.C.S.*, p. 322: *De Or.*, 27, 10; Methodius, *The Symposium of the Ten Virgins*, IX, 3. Hippolytus draws a parallel between Eve driven from the tree of life in Paradise and Mary Magdalen laying hold of Jesus in the garden (*Com. Cant.*, 15; *G.C.S.* 351–2). One may ask whether the *Epistle to Diognetus* does not make an allusion to the same theme (12, 8); and it is possible that the account in John 20. 11–18 of the appearing to Magdalen may have a reference both to the garden of Paradise and to baptism.[15] This assimilation of Christ to the tree of life pointed the way to the likening of Christians to the trees of Paradise.[16]

Side by side with the paradise motif is found that of "the tree planted (πεφυτευμένον) by running water" of Psalm 1. 3. This is often identified with the Word, as by Asterius the Sophist: "The Word is the tree planted by the water's edge which the Father has begotten without intermediary, laden with fruit (εὔκαρπον, πολυφόρον),

[14] On this text, see J. Daniélou, "Das Leben das am Holze hängt", in *Festgabe Geiselmann* (Freiburg, 1960), pp. 28–9.

[15] R. Mercurio, "A Baptismal Motif in the Gospel Narratives of the Burial", in *C.B.Q.*, 21 (1959), p. 52.

[16] See also Eusebius, *Com. Psalm.* 1. 3 (*P.G.*, 23, 77B–C): the Christian planted in Paradise is assimilated to the tree of life which is Christ; Didymus, *Com. Psalm.* 1. 3 (*P.G.*, 39, 1157C).

flourishing (εὐθαλές), tall (ὑψίκομον), fair-branched (καλλίκλωνον). . . . It was of this tree that Adam refused the fruit and fell victim to its opposite. Christ is the tree of life, the devil the tree of death" (*Hom.*, I, 4–5: Richard, p. 2).[17] This symbolism appears also in Justin (*I Apol.*, XL, 7–9; *Dial.*, LXXXVI, 4) and Clement of Alexandria (*Strom.*, V, 11, 72, 2). But the tree can also stand for the soul, as in Didymus in relation to baptism: "I will send my Spirit on those who know not baptism and walk in waterless places (Is. 44. 3), my Spirit who will enable the font (κολυμβήθρα) to make them blossom (ἀναθῆλαι) like the water-plants, like the tree planted by the waterside."[18] We call to mind the theme of the tree by the water's edge in the *Hodayoth*, which may have been influenced by Psalm I. 3.

This baptismal theme indeed goes back to Judaic Christianity. It can be found in a remarkable passage of Pseudo-Barnabas: "Let us look whether the Lord has been careful to tell us about the water and the cross before-hand. . . . Through another prophet, he says again: 'He who does these things shall be like a tree planted close to water, giving its fruit in due season . . . .' Notice how he describes the water and the cross together, for what he means to say is, 'Happy are they who, putting their hope in the cross, have gone down into the water.' . . . After-wards it is said that 'there was a river flowing from the right-hand side, and beautiful trees grew from it; and he who shall eat of them will live for ever.'[19] That is to say

---

[17] See P. Salmon, *Les Tituli Psalmorum des anciens psautiers latins* (Rome, 1959), pp. 81, 121, 138, 153.

[18] *Trin.*, II, 12; *P.G.*, 39, 556A. See also *Com. Psalm.* I. 3; *P.G.*, 39, 1157C.

[19] This refers to Ez. 47, but not in a literal way. It is a sort of Judaeo-Christian *targum* of Ezechiel, analogous to that found in Apoc. 22. 2. See Windisch, *Der Barnabasbrief* (Tübingen, 1920), pp. 368–9.

that we go down into the water full of sin and defilement, but we come up out of it bearing fruit (καρποφοροῦντες)" (XI, 1–11). Here the tree of Psalm 1. 3 points to those whom baptism has made like the Word. It is the same with the trees that grow near the eschatological river in Ezechiel 47, they are the baptized, bearing fruit.[20]

Moreover, it appears that this group of ideas goes back to Judaism itself. In his *Jewish Symbols in the Graeco-Roman Period* (VII, p. 127), Goodenough says that, perhaps since Ezechiel, the trees of Paradise are the just themselves, for the image, familiar since Proverbs, according to which they were like trees planted by the water-brooks, laden with fruit and always green, becomes in the *Psalms of Solomon* the godly ones of the Lord who are said to have life for ever through the Law.[21] In any case the exegesis of Barnabas certainly seems to imply a Jewish exegesis of Ez. 47 which interpreted the trees of life growing by the living waters as the just men of the messianic age. The Qumran texts we have quoted seem equally to rest on this grouping of Old Testament passages.

So we see the affinities of the three themes, the φυτεία as a symbol of the Church, the tree as a figure of the baptized person, the tree of life as a figure of Christ. But, as Bertil Gärtner has clearly seen (*op. cit.*, p. 27), this all belongs to a single symbolical whole, which goes back to pre-Christian Judaism and Judaeo-Christianity. It comprises a number of biblical overtones, of which the chief are the description of Paradise in Genesis 2, chapter 47 of Ezechiel and the beginning of Psalm 1. These are all very important passages among the *testimonia* of primitive

[20] The baptismal exegesis of Ps. 1. 3 is found again in Gregory of Nyssa, *In bapt.*; P.G., 46, 593D–596A.

[21] There may be cited in particular Prov. 11. 28; Ps. 1. 3; 51. 10 (= 52. 8); 91. 13; Jer. 17. 8.

Christianity. Already combined in pre-Christian Judaism with the rivers of Eden and the Jordan, the whole formed part of the primitive catechesis: it was brought into direct relation with baptism, as the term "neophyte" shows. It presents a remarkable theology of the Church, planted by Christ and the apostles, baptism being the planting in it and the tree of life its centre.

In Isaias 5. 1–7 the vine of Yahweh, symbolizing the Israelite people, is a vineyard (ἀμπελών). Here is the plantation again, but of grape-vines (ἄμπελοι) rather than trees. Notice in verse 7 that the word νεόφυτον is equivalent to ἀμπελών in designating the plantation. It is the theme that Christ takes up in Matthew 21. 33–41, and is found again in Judaeo-Christian writings. In Hermas, for example: his fifth parable is that of the vineyard: "God planted the vineyard (ἀμπελών), that is, he brought his people into being and entrusted it to his Son" (v, 6, 2). And again in v, 5, 2: "The vines are the people which he planted"; here each plant represents a Christian.[22]

But along with this there goes another theme, that of the whole people of Israel as a vine-plant (ἄμπελος).[23] This is found in Psalm 79. 9. Israel is a vine (ἄμπελος) which God planted (κατεφύτευσας);[24] it filled the land, "the shadow of it covered the hills, and the branches thereof the cedars of God" (11). Again, in Ezechiel 17. 1–8. As with the plantation, the plant need not be a vine-stock. In *Hodayoth*, VI, 15–16 it is a *nezer*, a shoot,

[22] See also *Mand.*, X, 1, 5, and *Sim.*, IX, 26, 3–4.

[23] Clement of Alexandria calls the Church "the Lord's vine (ἀμπελών)" (*Strom.*, VII, 12, 74, 1). We have met the expression before, in the *Apostolic Constitutions*, Praef.

[24] See Justin, *Dial.*, CX, 4: "The vine planted by Christ, God and Saviour, is his people."

a sucker: "The *nezer* will spread its shade over all the earth, its top will touch the sky and its roots go down to the abyss."[25] The parable in Matthew 13. 32 is in the same line. The image of the birds nesting in the branches of the great tree is found also in Ezechiel 17. 23, Daniel 4. 9 and *Midrash of Habacuc*, VIII, 9.

In John 15. 1–7 the theme of the Church as a plant takes a special form: "I am the true vine, and my Father is the husbandman. . . . I am the vine, you the branches (κλήματα)." It is likely that Jesus was here applying to himself the image of the vine (ἄμπελος) as standing for Israel. He is the true Israel. But the emphasis is on the fact that the true Israel is formed by the union of Christ, who is the stem, with the branches, who are the members. It is a variant of St Paul's theme of the union of head and members. But here again an element from the *Hodayoth* may, perhaps, have come in. We have just seen that there was question therein of the *nezer*, shoot, of Isaias 11.1. This sprang from the trees of life (*Hod.*, VIII, 6) and grew into a huge forest (VI, 15). Bertil Gärtner inclines to interpret the word in a collective sense, designating the community (*op. cit.*, p. 22). We should then have a variant of the vine or tree representing Israel. But it could also have an individual sense, and refer to the Messiah to come or the Master of Justice. It is then the plant from which the community grows, and this would be an anticipation of John's theme.

In any case this theme occurs in Judaic Christianity. Ignatius of Antioch in his *Letter to the Trallians*, XI, 2, after speaking of "the Father's planting", goes on: "If they were [planted by him], they would appear as branches (κλάδοι)

[25] For the *nezer*, see B. Gärtner, *op. cit.*, p. 24; he suggests that the word Ναζωραῖος could have reference to *nezer*.

of the cross, and their fruit would be imperishable. Christ in his passion calls you by his cross, you who are his members: the head cannot come to birth alone without members." Here we pass from the theme of the plantation to that of the tree, as in *Hodayoth*, VI, 15–16; it is not a matter of vine and shoots (κλῆμα) but of tree and boughs (κλάδος). The image is independent of John. The tree is assimilated to the cross.[26] We have met a similar assimilation in Justin, with regard to the tree planted by the water. From the fact that its fruit is imperishable (ἄφθαρτος), it appears that the cross is here considered as "tree of life".[27] And the parallel with the figure of head and members clearly shows that we have an equivalent of John's theme of the vine, and that the meaning is the same.

The union of the vine with its shoots or of the trunk with its branches as a symbol of the union of Christ and the Church, as well as the figure of the plantation, is found to have been part of the catechesis. Under John's form of the vine, it appears in Hippolytus: "The spiritual vine (ἄμπελος) was the Saviour. The shoots (κλήματα) and vine-branches are his saints, those who believe in him. The bunches of grapes are his martyrs; the trees which are joined with the vine show forth the Passion; the vintagers are the angels; the baskets full of grapes are the apostles; the winepress is the Church; and the wine is the power of the Holy Spirit" (*Ben. Isaac*; *P.O.*, 27, p. 99).[28]

A homily of Zeno of Verona is more interesting still, for it is a mystagogical catechesis for neophytes: "The

[26] That this is a Judaeo-Christian theme is now confirmed by its presence in Palestinian inscriptions. See B. Bagatti, "Una pagina inedita sulla Chiesa primitiva di Palestina", in *Oss. Rom.* (6 August 1960), p. 4.

[27] See Justin, *Dial.*, LXXXVI, 1. I leave aside the theme of the cross, which I have examined elsewhere (*Théologie du judéo-christianisme*, pp. 289–316).

[28] See also Clement of Alexandria, *Quis dives*, 37, 6.

parable of the vine, dear brothers, requires to be expounded at length." The reference is to Isaias 5. 1–7, read during the paschal vigil at that time. "The Lord's vine was the former synagogue, which ... produced sour grapes instead of sweet. Wroth at that, the Lord ... planted another, one conformable to his will, our mother the Church. He tended it through the labours of his priests ...; and having suspended it on the blessed wood, he trained it to bear an abundant harvest. And so today among your number, new shoots are trained along their trellises; bubbling like a sweet stream of fermenting must, they have filled the Lord's wine-vault to the great joy of all" (*Tract.*, II, 28; *P.L.*, II, 471–2). Here, to symbolize baptism, the figure of the shoot grafted on to the stock takes the place of the plant planted in the paradise.

In another mystagogical catechesis, of Asterius the Sophist this time, we find: "The divine and timeless vine has sprung from the grave, bearing as fruits (ἐκαρποφόρησεν) the newly baptized (νεοφωτίστους), like bunches of grapes (βότρυας) on the altar. ... The vine has been harvested, and the altar loaded with fruit like a winepress. Today vine-dressers, vintagers, gatherers, singing cicadas, have again shown us the paradise of the Church in all her beauty. Who are the vine-dressers? The prophets and the apostles. ... And who the cicadas? The newly baptized, bathed in dew as they come from the font, resting— as it were—on the cross as against a tree, warmed by the sun of justice, shining with the Spirit and carolling spiritual songs" (*Hom.*, XIV, 1–2; Richard, p. 105).

Manifold are the themes interwoven in this lyrical passage: the Church–Paradise, the wood of the cross, the mystical winepress. But what interests us is the theme of Christ: the pre-existing vine which bears grapes, the neophytes. Then they become cicadas; but we are used to these changes of level. It is noteworthy that the theme of the vine as a figure of the Church occurs elsewhere in Asterius: "It would be preposterous that, whereas those who go into a natural vineyard (ἀμπελών) do not tire of picking good fruit from each stem (ἄμπελος) ..., we, going into that noble paradise where the only-begotten Vine spreads out apostolic shoots and bears patriarchal clusters, should not be insatiable in gathering what befits us, though the vine flourishes more in the very harvesting" (*Hom.* I, 8; see also XVI, 1–6).

But it must be noticed that by the side of John's symbol of the vine, Asterius also keeps the Ignatian symbol of the tree of life: "Christ is the tree of life, the devil the tree of death. The one drives man from Paradise, the other introduces the thief into Paradise. It has the apostles for branches (κλάδους), those who are saved for fruit, words for leaves, baptism for root, the Father is the gardener" (*Hom.* I, 5). This is exactly Ignatius's image. Christ is the tree of life, the saved are its fruit; opposed to it stands the tree of death. This is the old Judaeo-Christian theme, parallel to that of the vine, persisting in the catechetical tradition and appearing anew in the lyricism of Asterius.

It was perhaps unnecessary to refer to pre-Christian Judaism. The themes of the vine and of the tree of life continued to live in Judaism, and the synagogue at Dura-Europos furnishes an example. There, above the niche of the Torah, is a tree-like form, in which Goodenough sees a vine. One thinks of the golden vine which was to be seen on the great gateway into Herod's Temple, and the vines depicted on Jewish coins. But Kraeling points out that the plant in question does not show any grapes, and he inclines to see it rather as the tree of life. If that be right, the representation would relate to the eschatological hope.[29] In the first case the reference would probably be to the children of Israel; in the second, to the Messiah. The very ambiguity of the image, and the iconographic possibilities of the ambiguity, show to what a degree these two themes intermingled. And that is just what the homilies of Asterius show us.[30]

We reach the conclusion that, of the catechetical images of the Church—the temple, the ship, the flock—one of the most primitive is the plantation. It is found in its pure state in the oldest documents, which took it over from Judaism. It sometimes developed under the form of a paradisial garden, sometimes under the form of God's vineyard. This image has to be distinguished from that of Christ as the tree of life or as the vine-stock on which shoots and branches grow; this last image represents the close connection between Christ and his members in the Church. But from the *Hodayoth* of Qumran on, and from Ignatius of Antioch on, we find one metaphor passing into another. Finally that of the φυτεία, the plantation, tends to give place to that of the mystical vine.

Still, the theme of the Church planted by the apostles, which is found in the *Ascension of Isaias*, denoted a characteristic aspect of the Church. It is a missionary term which modern missionary language has rediscovered; we now again speak of "planting the Church". Clement of Alexandria's image of heathens transplanted into the Church's good soil, and there bearing fruit, retains all its

[29] *The Excavations of Dura-Europos: Final Report*, VIII, 1, pp. 62–5.
[30] See Didymus, *Com. Psalm.* 1. 3: "The true vine is the tree of life" (*P.G.*, 39, 1157C). With the Dura-Europos fresco may be compared that in the catacomb of Domitilla at Rome, which represents a large tree-like vine; see *D.A.C.L.*, s.v. "Vigne".

meaning for us today. Surely it was interesting to show that this new image has the authority of a very ancient tradition, and to restore the full significance of its associations to the word "neophyte". It is the application to a particular theme of the rediscovery of the great ecclesiological symbols of the patristic age.

3

Living Water and the Fish

Oscar Cullmann has pointed out that the expression
"living water" (ὕδωρ ζῶν) can be understood in four ways.
In its ordinary literal meaning it denotes spring-water,
running water, as distinct from standing water. In its
ritual sense it means baptismal water. In its biblical sense
it denotes God as the fountain-head or source of life.
In its Christian sense it symbolizes the Holy Spirit.[1]
These various meanings are not necessarily connected.
Every allusion to the Holy Spirit as the living water has
not of necessity a baptismal overtone. To refer to baptism
as the living water does not necessarily mean that it is
given in running water.

Nevertheless, there are normal "tie-ups" between these
different meanings. The symbolism of living water depends on the original, secular meaning of the term: that
is a fundamental point for any serious study of the symbolism. Furthermore, the symbolism of living water may
well have been the determining factor in its adoption for a
given ritual usage; and reciprocally, the ritual usage has
helped to develop the theological symbolism. We shall,
therefore, have to take these different aspects into account.
At the same time we do not forget that our principal
object is the symbolism of living water; the other elements
that we introduce are to help us to understand that.

We will begin with some observations about the ritual

[1] *Les Sacrements dans l'évangile johannique* (Paris, 1951), p. 22.

usage. There is a well-known text in the *Didache*, "Concerning baptism, baptize thus, in the name of the Father and of the Son and of the Holy Spirit, in living water (ἐν ὕδατι ζῶντι)" (VII, 1). J.-P. Audet believes that this passage belongs to the earliest redaction of the document. What follows—concerning the use of other sorts of water in default of living water—he attributes to an interpolator, but of a not much later date.[2] The procedure laid down by the *Didache* is confirmed by other ancient texts. The New Testament affords no explicit testimony; but the *Apostolic Tradition* speaks of "clean running water" for baptism. The primitive Judaeo-Christian character of the usage is attested by the pseudo-Clementine *Homilies and Recognitions* (*Rec.*, 3, 67; VI, 15).[3]

The term "living water" applies to various waters. Fundamentally it denotes any water from a spring or source, but it also indicates water of a brook or a river, and the pseudo-Clementine writings point to frequent baptisms in the sea. Theodor Klauser has shown that living water could also be water carried through a conduit to flow into a basin or pool.[4] This must have been the most common, as we see from the Lateran baptistery, where the water flowed from the mouths of seven bronze stags' heads.

The ritual use of living water has a very wide context. It is found in Graeco-Roman religions. But more particularly it is found in Judaism. The Old Testament mentions it, for purifications, in Leviticus (14. 5). Above all, Judaism at the time of Christ gives evidence of the

---

[2] *La Didachè, Instructions des Apôtres* (Paris, 1958), pp. 358–67.

[3] See J. Daniélou, *Théologie du judéo-christianisme*, pp. 378–9.

[4] See his "Taufet in lebendigem Wasser", in *Pisciculi* (Münster, 1939), pp. 157–60.

importance given to rites in which living water had a chief part. The Mandaeans make living water the essential rite (*Ginza*, II, 1, 180). John the Baptist baptizes in the river Jordan. The *Sibylline Oracles* (IV, 165; *G.C.S.*, p. 100) prescribe bathing the whole body in "streams of living water" (ἀενάοισιν). The Elkesaites recommend against rabies a bath "in a deep river or spring" (Hippolytus, *Elench.*, IX, 15, 4). Proselytes to Judaism are baptized in living water, which is enjoined also for purifications.[5]

So the ritual context of living water is that of Judaeo-Christianity, with which it is connected. But there is a theological context as well. In the Old Testament living water is a symbol of God as the source of life. Thus in Jeremias 2. 13: "They have forsaken me, the fountain of living water (ὕδατος ζωῆς)." The Song of Songs (4. 15) speaks of "the well of living waters" (ὕδατος ζῶντος), no doubt in a symbolical sense. In Ezechiel and Zacharias this living water denotes the eschatological outpouring of God's life. We may quote Zacharias 14. 8: "Living waters (ὕδωρ ζῶν) shall go out from Jerusalem."

But this eschatological outpouring is more particularly associated with the Holy Spirit, as appears already in Ezechiel 36. 25–7. The relationship of baptism in water and baptism in the Holy Spirit mentioned in connection with John the Baptist in Matthew 3. 11 certainly seems to refer to Ezechiel, who also distinguishes two steps and associates the water with the cleansing which precedes the gift of the Spirit.[6] This linking is found again in the Qumran *Manual of Discipline*, IV, 21.

But another Qumran document seems rather to

[5] See J. Thomas, *Le Mouvement baptiste en Palestine et en Syrie* (Gembloux, 1955).
[6] G. W. H. Lampe, *The Seal of the Spirit*, p. 28.

assimilate the living water to the Torah, and this is found also in the Talmud.[7] This is in *Hymn O* (col. 8), where the Master of Justice is represented as giving living water:[8]

> I give you thanks, Adonai,
> for you have set me like a river-head
> in a parched land,
> like a gush of water in a waterless land.

Further on there is question of the Shoot, whose

> source will have access to living waters
> and will become an everlasting fountain.

Then it is said that

> he shall not drink at the source of life.

And,

> There has been thought of, but no belief in,
> the source of life.

Finally the elect

> will flow like rivers of unfailing waters.
> You have opened their fount by my hand.

John in his gospel has inherited the symbolism of living water; he is the only New-Testament writer who makes use of the expression ὕδωρ ζῶν. A first passage is the one about the woman of Samaria: "'If thou didst know the gift of God ... thou perhaps wouldst have asked of him, and he would have given thee living water (ὕδωρ ζῶν).' The woman saith to him: 'Sir, thou hast nothing wherein to draw, and the well is deep. From whence then hast thou living water? ...' Jesus answered and said to her:

[7] Strack-Billerbeck, II, pp. 433–6.
[8] The translations are from the French of A. Dupont-Sommer.

'Whosoever drinketh of this water shall thirst again; but he that shall drink of the water that I will give him shall not thirst for ever. But the water that I will give him shall become in him a fountain of water, springing up into life everlasting'" (4. 10–14). It may be remarked, with Father F.-M. Braun,[9] that the contrast between Jacob's well and the living water given by Christ could betoken the contrast between the Law and the Gospel, for in the *Damascus Document* (VI, 4) the well indicates the Law and, besides, living water is a symbol of the Law. The parallel with *Hymn O* is striking.

On the other hand St John records these words of Christ: "If any man thirst, let him come to me and drink, he that believeth in me. As the scripture saith, Out of his belly shall flow rivers of living water. Now this he said of the Spirit which they should receive who believed in him" (7. 37–9). Here, living water is a symbol of the Holy Spirit. Notice that this is John's own comment and it rests on his theology. This symbolism reappears at the end of the Apocalypse: "And he shewed me a river of water of life ($\H{v}\delta\omega\rho$ $\zeta\omega\hat{\eta}s$) . . . proceeding from the throne of God and of the Lamb" (22. 1). We have seen that the *Manual of Discipline* is the first text in which living water figures in direct association with the Holy Spirit. For Ezechiel and John the Baptist they are dissociated as two steps. It may then be thought that the symbolism of living water as representing the Holy Spirit is properly John's, and in him depends on the theology of Qumran.

There is still one last observation to make. It has been suggested,[10] and it is probable, that the two passages we

[9] "L'Arrière-fond judaïque du quatrième Évangile et la communauté de l'Alliance", in *R.B.*, 62 (1955), pp. 24–6.

[10] By O. Cullmann, *op. cit.*, pp. 50–4, 58–61.

have quoted from John have sacramental overtones. It is the baptismal outpouring of the Holy Spirit that is being pointed to. This is of capital importance. For it makes John the first writer explicitly to connect the two themes we have studied—the Judaeo-Christian rite of baptism in living water and the symbolism of living water as denoting the Holy Spirit. It is with him that the living water of the baptismal rite explicitly indicates the outpouring of the Holy Spirit. Here we have a theology of baptism, and one distinct from St Paul's theology which is more concerned with the likening to the dead and risen Christ symbolized by immersion and emersion.

This unity of the rite of living water with the symbolism of living water is found in the *Odes of Solomon*, if it be admitted, with J. H. Bernard, that they have a baptismal character. Thus, in XI, 6: "Speaking waters touched my lips from the fountain of the Lord plenteously: and I drank and was inebriated with the living water that doth not die." The expression "speaking water" occurs also in Mandaean texts.[11] And there is Ignatius of Antioch to be remembered: "There is a living water ($ὕδωρ$ $ζῶν$) within me, which whispers, 'Come to the Father'" (*Rom.*, VII, 2). Zeno of Verona, too, speaks of the soft murmuring of the living water (*Tract.*, II, 35); this seems to be an allusion to the low sound that running water makes.

In addition, Ode XXX is a call to the baptized in the same terms: "Fill ye waters for yourselves from the living fountain of the Lord . . . and come, all ye thirsty, and take the draught; and rest by the fountain of the Lord" (1–2). There will be noticed in this text the resemblances to Isaias 55. 1: "All you that thirst, come to the waters",[12]

---

[11] E. Segelberg, *Masbûtâ*, p. 45.

[12] Found again in Apoc. 21. 6: "To him that thirsteth, I will give of the fountain of the water of life ($τοῦ$ $ὕδατος$ $τῆς$ $ζωῆς$), freely."

and to Psalm 22. 2, "He gives me a resting-place where there is green pasture, leads me out to the cool water's brink."[13] It is difficult to think that the *Odes of Solomon* depend on John, but on the other hand their connection with the Qumran writings is certain. They represent a parallel development whose context is Judaeo-Christian.

So far we have been unravelling the essential elements of the material sign and of the spiritual reality which constitute the symbolism of living water. But it is possible yet more to clarify the *Sitz im Leben*, the biblical context of this symbolism. A few remarks about the texts we have quoted will help us in this.

After having described the stream of living water flowing from the eschatological Temple, the beginning of Apocalypse, ch. 22, goes on: " ... on both sides of the river was the tree of life, bearing twelve fruits, yielding its fruits every month; and the leaves of the tree were for the healing of the nations." *Odes of Solomon*, XI, after mentioning the speaking water, adds: "Blessed, O Lord, are they who ... have a place in thy Paradise; and they grow according to the growth of thy trees" (15–16). In the Qumran *Hymn O* (col. 8, 5–6) the trees of life go with the water of life.

In these texts the fountain of living water, the plantation of trees of life and the theme of the Temple are brought together. This directs our attention to our first passage, Ezechiel, ch. 47. In the description of the eschatological Temple we read: "Behold, waters issued out from under the threshold of the house . . . . It was a torrent which

[13] See Apoc. 7. 17, "The Lamb . . . shall rule them and shall lead them to the fountains of the waters of life ($\dot{v}\delta\acute{a}\tau\omega\nu\ \zeta\omega\hat{\eta}s$)."

I could not pass over. . . . By the torrent on the banks thereof on both sides shall grow all trees that bear fruit: their leaf shall not fall off and their fruit shall not fail. Every month shall they bring forth first-fruits, because the waters thereof shall issue out of the sanctuary" (1–12). The stream of living water flowing from the Temple fertilizes trees of life, which are the renewed Paradise. This theme unquestionably inspired John's Apocalypse (22. 1–2) and the *Odes of Solomon* (VI, 7).[14]

The allusion to this passage of Ezechiel and evidence for its early application to baptism appear in a passage in the *Epistle of Barnabas* which is one of those mosaics of biblical quotations that are characteristic of Judaeo-Christianity.[15] It runs: "And then, what says the prophet? 'There was a river flowing from the right-hand side, and beautiful trees grew (ἀνέβαινε) from it; and he who shall eat of them will live for ever.' That is to say that we go down into the water full of sin and defilement, but we come up out of it bearing fruit in our hearts, dread and hope in Jesus, being in the Spirit" (XI, 10–11). We notice the correspondence with John 6. 52: "If any man eat of this bread, he shall live for ever," and with Apocalypse 2. 7: "I will give [him] to eat of the tree of life." The midrash quoted by Barnabas seems to bring these two texts together, which implies an assimilation of the Eucharist to the fruit of the tree of life.

Pictorial monuments confirm the written evidence. Mosaics in baptisteries often depict the baptismal spring of living water surrounded by the trees of life. P. A. Underwood has shown[16] that in the fifth century Christ's tomb

[14] See the note in Bernard, *op. cit.*, p. 56. There is an explicit reference to "the brook that becomes a torrent".

[15] See *Théologie du judéo-christianisme*, pp. 102–11, and page 33, above.

[16] "The Fountain of Life", in *Dumbarton Oaks Papers*, 51 (1950), pp. 96–9.

appears as a fountain gushing living water. The tomb is also the new Paradise, and the cross represents the tree of life. These developments bring in new themes, but they are in prolongation of Ezechiel's words.

The important point here is the connection between the living water and the trees of life, and this connection underlines a new aspect of living water. It is not simply running water as distinct from standing water. It is water which gives life, in opposition to waters that bring death.[17] Following this line, the passage from Ezechiel will help us to understand the meaning of another symbol, namely, the fish. It is well known that in ancient Christian symbolism the fish stands for the Christian. Following the Latin Fathers, this is generally explained by the fact that ἰχθύς, fish, is the acrostic of "Jesus Christ, Son of God, Saviour". But on the other hand the fish generally appears in a baptismal context. Thus Tertullian: "But we, little fish, are born in water" (*Bapt.*, 1, 3); and Ambrose: "It has been reserved for you that water should bring you forth to grace, as it brought forth other [living beings] to natural life. Imitate this fish . . ." (*Sacram.*, III, 1, 3).[18] Paintings in the catacombs often testify to this connection of the fish with the baptismal water.

The connection is older than Christianity. Goodenough shows the place it held in Jewish art, where water is represented full of fish, which signify the resurrection.[19] This brings us back to living water, which is that in which there are living things: so the presence of fish in it signifies that the water is living water. And that is just what is

[17] The expression ὕδωρ ζωῆς stresses this aspect, while ὕδωρ ζῶν indicates running water.

[18] See also the inscriptions of Abercius and of Pectorius.

[19] *Jewish Symbols*, v, pp. 36–61.

found in Ezechiel 47, where we read concerning the torrent flowing from the Temple: "These waters that issue forth ... to the east and go down to the plains of the desert, shall go into the sea ... and the waters shall be healed. And every living creature that creepeth whithersoever the torrent shall come shall live; and there shall be fishes in abundance. ... And the fishers shall stand over these waters" (8–10).

When we reflect on the part played by this chapter of Ezechiel in the theology of living water, it seems clear that the baptismal symbolism of the fish is equally connected with it, as Allgeier saw.[20] The fish denotes the Christian quickened by the outpouring of eschatological water which has its source in Jerusalem. The passage suggests other themes. The sea to the east of Jerusalem, which is healed by the living water, is the Dead Sea. Confronted by a water in which nothing lives, living water acquires its full value, and it is obvious how much the symbol could mean to people dwelling near the Dead Sea. In the same way, for John the Baptist the Jordan before it falls into the Dead Sea became the sign of living water. We notice, too, that fishermen are associated with water that lives, i.e., that is full of fish. Its baptismal significance in early Christian art is beyond doubt, and this too may have been suggested to the Christianity of those days by the passage in Ezechiel. Edwin Hoskyns suggested this with reference to John 21. 1–14; and it could be true also for Luke 5. 1–11.[21]

We discern at once the importance of the passage from

[20] "Vidi aquam", in *Römische Quartalschrift*, 39 (1931), pp. 29 ff.

[21] *The Fourth Gospel* (London, 1947), p. 554.—In these texts it is not the Dead Sea but the Lake of Genesareth that is full of fish. But it must be noted that in the Septuagint the waters that flow from the Temple are said to "spread into Galilee" (Ez. 47. 8).

Ezechiel for the origin of the Christian symbolism of living water. The passage accounts for the importance of this symbolism in the Qumran documents, in John's writings and in the *Odes of Solomon*. It explains the presence of the dependent themes—the paradise of trees of life, the fish in the water. This does not exclude the influence of other relevant Old-Testament texts, which we shall have to refer to; but we are entitled to say that the influence of the Ezechiel text was preponderant.[22]

There is confirmation of this in a collection of *testimonia* which goes under the name of Gregory of Nyssa. Among those relating to baptism is a quotation from Ezechiel 47. But this has characteristic modifications, which show its relationship with the ancient dossier of *testimonia* for which the *Epistle of Barnabas* provides evidence, and also its application to baptism: "This water, spreading into Galilee, will hallow (ἁγιάσει) the waters, and every soul (ψυχή) to whom this water shall come will live and be healed (ἰαθήσεται)" (*P.G.*, 46, 232A). This is a shortened form of Ezechiel 47. 8–9, but several modifications are characteristic. The word ὑγιάσει, "heal", is replaced by ἁγιάσει, "hallow"; πᾶσα ψυχὴ τῶν ζῴων, which means "living creatures", is reduced to πᾶσα ψυχή, "every soul". The fact that the fish are called πᾶσα ψυχή makes the transition easier.

There is still one element of Ezechiel's text to be clarified: the waters flow *from the temple*. This occurs also in John's Apocalypse, and it is a constitutive element of the theme. What is this association of the Temple with living water to be connected with? John's gospel 7. 37 may be relevant here: it was in the Temple that Jesus proclaimed himself

---

[22] See E. Peterson, *Frühkirche, Judentum und Gnosis* (Freiburg, 1959), pp. 323–7.

to be the fount of living water. His words were spoken against a background of the feast of Tabernacles. Now one of the rites of this feast was a libation of water. Is there reason to suppose that this pouring out of water in the Temple was looked on as the figure of the eschatological pouring out of living water in Ezechiel?[23]

Here it may be recalled that there is an Old-Testament passage depending on Ezechiel, in which the image of the eschatological torrent flowing from Jerusalem is brought into association with the feast of Tabernacles as a figure of the eschatological mustering: the text is Zach. 14. 8 ff. There we have the living water (ὕδωρ ζῶν) issuing from Jerusalem and flooding towards both east and west, and also the nations going up to Jerusalem for the feast of Tabernacles (verse 16). We know that this feast had been given an eschatological meaning, and consequently it was normal that the libations of living water should be seen as the figure of the outpouring of God's life, conceived as a river of living water.

As J. Comblin has made clear,[24] Christ's utterance receives full significance when considered in this way: "As the scripture saith, Out of his belly shall flow rivers of living water." The scripture appealed to is that of Zacharias, the only Old-Testament text in which ὕδωρ ζῶν has an eschatological sense. For Ezechiel—and Zacharias who depends on him—the living water springs from beside the Temple; and therefore Christ, looking on himself as the temple of the New Covenant, applies the prophecy to himself. We know that this is a theme dear to St John.

[23] See J. Daniélou, "Le Symbolisme eschatologique de la fête des Tabernacles", in *Irénikon*, 31 (1958), pp. 19–40.

[24] "La Liturgie de la Nouvelle Jérusalem", in *E.T.L.*, 29 (1953), pp. 29–33.

Thus the image takes on its fullest import. The pouring out of water in the Temple at the feast of Tabernacles is the figure of the eschatological pouring out of divine life. And this prophecy is fulfilled when Christ, who is the eschatological temple, declares at the feast of Tabernacles that the living water flows from his own side.

Round this kernel the theme of living water has gathered echoes of various Old-Testament episodes which have a literary relation to it; these must now be brought together, following a regressive order. We started from the fact of baptism as an outpouring of living water signifying an outpouring of the Spirit. We saw that this was the fulfilment of prophecies foretelling the eschatological outpouring of living water. But the prophecies in their turn have their starting-point in Old-Testament things, which are recalled in order to show in them in the past the figure or type of the greater things which God will bring about in the future. We have glanced at some of these themes in passing, but it is worth while referring to them again in order to bring out diverse harmonics in the living-water symbolism.

The first is the primordial waters of Genesis 1. 2, 20. These fertile waters are related to the theme of living water in as much as they brought forth living beings. That is a characteristic feature of baptismal typology. Tertullian wrote: "The first waters were commanded to bring forth living creatures . . . so there is no need to be surprised that in baptism water again produces life" (*Bapt.*, III, 4). It is interesting, especially for the theology of images, to notice how God familiarizes man with his way of acting in lesser matters in order to make more acceptable the deeds which will be accomplished in Christ. Ambrose quotes Genesis 1. 20, "Let the waters produce moving things that have life", and shows it to be a figure of baptism, in the text quoted above (page 50). The theme common to both waters is the fish.

The second figure is that of Paradise, which is directly evoked by the passage of Ezechiel taken up by St John. The connecting link here is the trees of life. The river of living water will be a source of life to the new Paradise, as the four rivers were to the first. This is one aspect of the general theme of baptism as the return to Paradise, which was so important in ancient catechesis, particularly Syrian catechesis;[25] we have met it in the *Odes of Solomon*. The decoration of early Christian baptisteries provides noteworthy evidence of this, as D. de Bruyne and J. Quasten have pointed out.

A typical feature of this symbolism is the identification of the four rivers with the four gospels. Cyprian writes: "The Church, like Paradise, includes fruit-bearing trees within her walls. She waters the trees from four rivers, which are the four gospels, by which she dispenses the grace of baptism through a heavenly and saving stream" (*Epist.*, 73, 10). The same theme appears in Hippolytus (*Com. Dan.*, I, 17; *G.C.S.*, pp. 28 ff.), and it is taken up by Jerome (*Com. Mat.*, *Prol.*; *P.L.*, 26, 18A). P. A. Underwood has studied its development in Christian art (*art. cit.*, pp. 71–80, 118–31). This reminds us that in Jewish symbolism living water could signify the teaching of the Law. The Qumran *Hymn O* says: "You, O God, have put in my mouth this fountain of living water which will never dry up" (col. 8, 16); and it appears also in the *Odes of Solomon* (XL, 4–5).

[25] J. Daniélou, "Catéchèse pascale et retour au Paradis", in *La Maison-Dieu*, 45 (1956), pp. 99–119.

A third theme is the rock in the wilderness. Its baptismal interpretation goes back to 1 Cor. 10. 4, which calls Christ the rock from which living water flows, and to John 7. 38–9. Among the Fathers, it is found in Justin, "a fount of living water which Christ has called forth in the desert" (*Dial.*, LXIX, 6), in Tertullian (*Bapt.*, IX, 3), in Cyprian (*Epist.*, 63, 8), in Gregory of Elvira (*Tract.*, XV; *P.L. Suppl.*, I, pp. 445–8). The Fathers established a parallelism between the rock and Christ's utterance at the feast of Tabernacles, and this presupposes that the rock in the wilderness and the rock of the Temple are assimilated to one another. Moreover, the water which came out of Christ's side on the cross, in the setting of the typology of Exodus, which is that of John's gospel, is seen as the renewal of the water which flowed from the rock (Gregory of Elvira, *op. cit.*). This wealth of doctrine has been expounded by Hugo Rahner and F.-M. Braun.[26]

In the typology of the rock of the Exodus, the water in question is one which quenches thirst. This appears again in the episode of the Samaritan woman and in John 7. 37: "If any man thirst, let him come to me and drink, he that believeth in me." That is just what we find in the *Odes of Solomon*: "All the thirsty upon earth were given to drink of it" (VI, 10). Here is a new note in the theme of living water. It is not only life-giving for the fishes, not only fertilizing for the trees: it is also drinkable by men, it gives life to them too.[27] As J. H.

[26] Hugo Rahner, "Flumina de ventre Christi", in *Biblica*, 22 (1941), pp. 269–302, 367–403; F.-M. Braun, "L'eau et l'Esprit", in *R.T.*, 49 (1949), pp. 5–30.

[27] This corresponded to ritual usages. In Syria the liturgy of initiation included a cup of blessed water (see J.-M. Hanssens, *La Liturgie d'Hippolyte* (Rome, 1959), pp. 159, 484). This is found also among the Mandaeans (Segelberg, *Masbûtâ*, p. 59); it indicates an Eastern origin.

Bernard has observed, the Jewish symbolism of living water constantly passes from one level of image to another. There is to be noticed, too, the parallelism in St John between ὕδωρ ζωῆς (Apoc. 7. 17) and ἄρτος ζωῆς (John 6. 48), which replaces the parallelism ὕδωρ ζωῆς (Apoc. 22. 1) and ξύλον ζωῆς (Apoc. 22. 2).

A fourth theme is that of the Jordan. Here the original connections with baptism are plain at the ritual level. John the Baptist baptized in the Jordan. And on the other hand the Jordan is the very picture of living water, a flowing river; and its significance is heightened by the contrast of the Dead Sea. It is therefore easy to understand that the Old-Testament events in which it plays a part— Josue's crossing of it, Naaman's bathing in it, the axe of Eliseus, the ascension of Elias—appear as figures of baptism. In Mandaeism "Jordan" becomes the name of all baptismal water, named from "great Jordan of living waters".[28]

This inquiry might well be prolonged into later times. Liturgical texts, patristic commentaries, figured monuments, would show to what a degree the theme of living water is at the heart of the theology of baptism. It is not the only one; other symbolisms suggest other aspects—death and resurrection, cleansing. But this one emphasizes one of the essential things: if living water signifies the Spirit, baptism confers the life of the Spirit. Nor is there need of another sacrament to complete it in this order. That is what Tertullian failed to recognize, and so did Gregory Dix in our day. Confirmation is *another* outpouring of the Spirit, by which the bishop associates the Christian with his apostolic mission.

[28] E. Segelberg, *Masbûtâ*, p. 38.

4

The Ship of the Church

The symbolism of the ship and its origins have been the
object of a number of studies. F. J. Dölger examined it in a
chapter of his *Sol Salutis* (2nd ed., pp. 272–87). E. Peterson
devoted a valuable note to it, first published in *Theologische
Zeitschrift*, 6 (1950), pp. 77–9 and reprinted with further
matter in *Frühkirche, Judentum und Gnosis*, pp. 92–6. This
called forth a reply from K. Goldammer, in *Theologische
Zeitschrift*, 6 (1950), pp. 232–7. His studies on the symbolism of the cross gave Hugo Rahner cause to return
several times to the theme of the Church as a ship, particularly in "Antenna Crucis, III; Das Schiff aus Holz", in
Zeitschrift für katholische Theologie, 66 (1942), pp. 197–227.[1]
Nevertheless, certain recent works have contributed fresh
material, which justifies taking up the subject once more.

The fact from which we can start is that the theme of the
ship as a figure of the Church formed part of the catechetical tradition. This has been established by G. Strecker
in his book on the pseudo-Clementine writings.[2] The comparison is made in Clement's letter to James at the beginning
of the *Homilies*: "The body of the Church as a whole is
like a great ship carrying men of many different origins
through a violent storm." There follows a long allegory,
in which God is the owner of the ship and Christ the pilot,

[1] Cf. Hugo Rahner, *Greek Myths and Christian Mystery*, London and New
York, 1963.
[2] *Das Judenchristentum in den Pseudo-Klementinen* (Berlin, 1958), pp. 105–6,
113.

the bishop is like the look-out man (πρωρεύς), the presbyters are the crew (ναῦται), the deacons the leading oarsmen, the catechists the stewards (ναυστολόγοι). The allegory is carried on by comparing the turbulent waves to the temptations of the world and the passengers to the various orders in the Church, with the relevant maritime parallels. Strecker shows that this comparison forms part of a document anterior to the *Grundschrift*, which he puts in the second half of the third century (but which doubtless is earlier) and that the comparison enters into the liturgy of ordination.

This is confirmed by a passage in a liturgical document, the *Apostolic Constitutions*, in the discourse which precedes the ordination of bishops: "When you assemble God's church, be like the pilot of a great ship and keep watch that the gatherings are conducted in orderly fashion. See that the deacons show the brethren to their places, as sailors do passengers. . . . See that the church is . . . turned toward the east, as is proper for a ship . . . ; that the doorkeepers stand at the men's entrances to guard them, and that the deaconesses are at the women's doors, as stewards" (ɪɪ, 57). The resemblances between the two passages incline one to think that the *Apostolic Constitutions* depend on the *Epistle of Clement*, inasmuch as the passage does not form part of the *Didascalia*. It represents, too, a more developed state.[3]

But the antiquity of the symbol is assured by a text which is nearly contemporary with the document used by the *Clementine Homilies*, the *Treatise on Antichrist* of Hippolytus of Rome. The symbol is the same, but the details of the allegory are different, in such a way that there is no

---

[3] On the meaning of the different functions, see H. Rahner, *Das Schiff aus Holz*, pp. 200-1.

question of dependence: we have here an earlier traditional theme, taking us back to the second century. This is the passage: "The sea is the world. The Church is like a ship, buffeted by the waves but not swamped, for she has with her her experienced pilot, Christ. Amidships she has the trophy of victory over death, for she carries Christ's cross with her. Her bow points east, her stern west, her keel is to the south. For her double rudder she has the two Testaments. Her rigging is stretched out like the charity of Christ, embracing the Church.[4] With her she carries stocks of living water, the regenerating bath. . . . On her either side are seamen, like guardian angels, who steer and look after the Church. The ladder rising upwards to the sailyard is an image of the sign of Christ's passion leading the faithful to climb up into Heaven. The ropes joined at the yard on the mast-head are like the orders of prophets, martyrs and apostles at rest in Christ's kingdom" (59).

In this passage we have, on the one hand, the same fundamental analogies as in those that we have given previously: the ship is the Church, it is turned eastward, Christ is the pilot; but the details of the allegory are different. In the *Homilies* and the *Constitutions* its character is catechetical and liturgical; here its bearings are eschatological. We observe in particular that the space above the yard is regarded as ἀνάπαυσις, the place of rest, while the ladder (κλῖμαξ) leading aloft is an image of the cross whereby believers raise themselves to Heaven. Thus the mast and rigging as a whole form as it were a cosmic ladder. As F. J. Dölger remarked,[5] Hippolytus' image recalls the ladder to Paradise in the *Passion of Perpetua*, 4, and the μηχανή of

[4] See Asterius, *Hom.*, xx, 19: "All have reefed the spreading sails (ἄρμενα) of charity."

[5] *Sol Salutis* (Münster, 1925), p. 278.

Ignatius of Antioch (*Eph.*, IX, I), which raises to the heights and is the cross.

Even though it is later in date, there is a passage of Epiphanius that can be associated with the first picture; Rahner does not refer to it, but Strecker does, rightly. Its context is more theological, but the general lines are the same: "God's holy Church is like a ship. Now, a ship is not built of a single kind of wood, but of several. The keel is all made of the same wood, though not in a single piece; the anchors are of a different wood; the internal revetments (περιτόναια), the deck-boards, the ribs (ἐγκοίλια), the deck-houses, the stem, the bulwarks, the side planks, the mast and rudder, the cleats and seating, the tiller and other things—together they form one whole made of various woods" (*Pan.*, LXI, 3, 4). The object of all this is to show that there are differing orders in the Church and that married people have their place therein. We are, then, close to the theme of the *Homilies*.

So this use of the ship to symbolize the Church certainly goes back to writers of the beginning of the third century. The question then arises: Does this symbolism go back to the Jewish tradition or does it depend on Greek symbolism? At first sight we should be inclined to look to the latter. Marine images are not common in the Bible, Israel was not a sea-going people; but such images were very familiar to the Greeks, who ranged the Mediterranean. Father Hugo Rahner has demonstrated how images from the *Odyssey* were taken up by Christian writers from Clement of Alexandria onwards. More precisely, the comparison of the State to a ship, the king being the pilot, was current in Greek literature, and it looks to us like a very close approximation to the themes of the Church as a ship whose pilot is the bishop. This much must be granted to Gold-ammer.

But, while it is certain that the comparison was in high favour with the Greeks, it is nevertheless not certain that it did not have Jewish antecedents. There are several possible lines of investigation. Every student turns first to the *Testaments of the Twelve Patriarchs*. We read in the *Testament of Nephtali*: "After seven days I again saw my father, who was standing on the shore of the sea of Jamnia and we were with him. And a ship appeared, sailing without crew or pilot. . . . The name on the ship was 'Jacob's Ship'. Our father said to us, 'Come, we will go on board our ship.' But when we had done so a violent storm and a frightful hurricane arose. Our father, who was holding the tiller, was separated from us, and we were blown out to sea. The ship was swamped, the waves pounded it, and it broke up. Joseph went off in a dinghy. We clung to nine planks; Levi and Judah were on the same one. We were carried to the ends of the earth. Levi, wearing sackcloth, prayed to the Lord. And when the wind dropped, the ship (σκάφος) smoothly made land. Our father came, and we rejoiced with one accord" (VI, 1–10).

M. Philonenko finds little coherence in this text.[6] But this is not obvious. That the broken ship should put itself together again is natural enough in a writing of this form, which is a dream and not an historical narrative. Joseph's departure in a dinghy brings out the separation of the Josephite tribes, Ephraim and Manasses, from the others. The dispersion of Israel makes one think that the piece dates from after A.D. 70. Levi's part as intercessor is in accordance with the place given him in the *Testaments*:

[6] *Les Interpolations chrétiennes des Testaments des XII Patriarches et les manuscrits de Qoumrân* (Paris, 1960), p. 55.

he is doubtless the priestly messiah who will gather dispersed Israel at the end of time. The allusion to Jamnia, which became important after the fall of Jerusalem, is a proof that the text could not be Essenian. M. de Jonge declares it is Christian, against Philonenko and Peterson.[7]

This seems to be confirmed by the double comparison that the text forces on us. In the first place there is a Hebrew *Testament of Nephtali* which recounts Nephtali's vision, but in a different form. It is about the dispersion of Israel, for which Joseph is made responsible. There is no intercession by Levi and no calming of a storm. It is an haggadic polemical work against Joseph, similar to what is found in the *Book of Jubilees*, which makes it tenable that this Testament is Essenian. (A fragment of a Hebrew *Testament of Nephtali* has been found at Qumran.) Here the atmosphere is one of purely Jewish polemics. It is plain, then, that the Hebrew *Testament* is anterior to the Greek. The latter is entirely without the wholly Jewish aspects of the Haggadah. It keeps only the ship and the wreck, to which it adds the storm as causing the wreck and the calming of it at Levi's prayer. That is the point which is stressed.

This brings us to the second parallel, Christian this time: the narrative of the calming of the tempest in Mark 6. 47–51, which was pointed out by Edwyn Hoskyns.[8] He starts from the metaphor of a storm to express tribulation, such as is found in Psalms 17. 16 and 92. 3. "It was, perhaps, familiarity with this metaphor which led the priestly historian to elaborate the story of Noah as a type of Israel overwhelmed, as it were, in their captivity, by the 'great floods' of Gentile oppression." He then cites the

[7] *The Testaments of the Twelve Patriarchs* (Assen, 1953), p. 57.
[8] *The Riddle of the New Testament* (London, 1958), p. 70.

Greek *Testament of Nephtali*: "The sequence is precisely that of the Psalms. Tumult and oppression pictured as a storm—intervention by God—peace." And he goes on: "Exactly the same sequence occurs in Mark. . . . It is difficult to think that this general Old Testament background was absent from the mind of the author of the gospel." Erik Peterson, for his part, emphasizes the importance of the theme of a storm calmed by prayerful intercession, and notes that this is adverted to in Tertullian's exegesis of the calming of the tempest. The theme seems to him to be properly Jewish (*op. cit.*, pp. 95–6).

It would appear that the essential trait here is that of the storm as signifying the eschatological trials from which only God's power can bring deliverance, and that deliverance obtained by the intercession of holy men. It is noteworthy that this theme reappears in the fourth century in Asterius, who made considerable use of Judaeo-Christian symbolism. He says in his *Homilies on the Psalms*: "When the universal (οἰκουμενικόν) shipwreck occurs, when life is drowned in the waves of ungodliness, in order that the Christian may not perish with the ungodly, David has given him—as it were an anchor of safety for a ship buffeted by the winds—the words of a psalm: so that, like a pilot turning his gaze to the sky, he cries out, 'Save me, Lord, for there is no righteous man'" (XXI, 17). A little before, Asterius has applied the same image to the apostles during Christ's passion: "When, during the Passion the world was tossed like a ship, . . . the pilot was nailed to the cross, the veil of the temple was rent like a sail, then the apostles, deprived of their leader and battered by the storm, cried out in chorus 'Save me, Lord, . . . for there is no righteous man'" (XX, 17).

If we seek to plot the stages of the theme, we reach these

conclusions. The Old Testament knew a symbolism of the rough sea as standing for eschatological trials, whether under a personal aspect or as Israel's adversities; so the ship could signify either an individual man or the Jewish people. This theme appears in Jewish apocalyptic writings. It is found under the individual form in the *Hodayoth* (D.S.T., VI, 22-4), or under the collective form (Hebrew *Testament of Nephtali*).

In the era of the New Testament the theme received a new importance. Jesus' preaching in Galilee and the prominence of the Lake of Tiberias gave a material setting for marine images. Furthermore, the theme of the twelve apostles in a ship, like that of the *Testaments* with their twelve patriarchs, came from apocalyptic literature; to this was added that of the just man's intercession amidst the storm, which was foreign to the Hebrew *Testament*.

It seems to us that it was in relation to this narrative, and not after all necessarily in literary dependence on the Greek gospels, that the Christian author of the *Testaments of the Twelve Patriarchs* entirely recast Nephtali's dream. He took the Hebrew text and gave it a new meaning. Retaining the Jewish literary *genre*, he uses Levi to represent Christ as the priestly messiah, calming the storm through prayer and bringing the new Israel, the Church, to the shores of the messianic kingdom. One can agree with Peterson that there is here a remote adumbration of the ship's being used to figure the Church.

But a point that strikes us about these texts is this: the ship is not presented as the means of salvation, but simply as that which is saved; it is not a symbol of hope. Could there be another line, connected with the Jewish environment, which brings out this aspect? Here we come upon a text that is important because of its date. In his *First Apology*, Justin gives a number of figures of the cross, among them the brazen serpent, the military standard, the plough and the ship's mast: "One cannot sail the seas unless the trophy that is called the sail (ἱστίον) is properly set on the ship" (LV, 3). Here the image is quite different. It is no longer a matter of a wrecked ship saved by heavenly intervention: it is the ship which is the means of salvation. Only it does not symbolize the Church, but the cross.

This seems wholly in accordance with primitive Christian symbolism, in which symbols of the cross had a considerable place. More especially as regards this passage from Justin, Palestinian archaeology provides remarkable confirmation. Among the symbols found in ancient Judaeo-Christian ossuaries are the plough and the standard; there is also the ship.[9] And this ship is just what we should expect, with the transverse yard on the mast giving it the form of a cross; in this way the ship with its rigging becomes a figure of the saving cross. This seems to be the oldest form of the ship's salvation symbolism. And it persisted, for even when the ship became identified with the Church, the mast remained a symbol of the cross. We shall see in a minute the reason, given by Justin, for the division of the ship's sail into eight parts.

This ship symbolism in Judaeo-Christian archaeology had all the more chance of being generally accepted in that it had antecedents. These have been studied by Goodenough.[10] The ship appears on pagan funerary monuments, Greek and Roman and also Egyptian, as a symbol of immortality, and on many rings and precious stones it

[9] See E. Testa, "Fruttuose ricerche archeologiche palestinesi", in *Osservatore Romano*, 25 September 1960, p. 6.
[10] *Jewish Symbols*, VIII, 2, pp. 157–65.

symbolizes hope, for a happy journey of the soul in this life and the next. There is, too, an Old-Testament event which is of the greatest significance here, namely, Noah's ark, as the instrument of eschatological deliverance. Philo of Alexandria had already brought the two themes together, seeing the ark as an image of the soul moving towards the life of blessedness.

But these are precisely the themes which are found among the primitive Christians. They adopted the symbolism of the ship as a sign of hope for eternity, just as we find it on the funerary monuments.[11] On the other hand, they reinterpreted the common symbols on heathen gems and rings in a Christian sense. Clement of Alexandria gives an example of this which is specially interesting to us. He distinguishes symbols that Christians can accept from those they must reject; and among the first he mentions "the dove (πελειάς), the fish (ἰχθύς), the ship running before a favourable wind (οὐριοδρομοῦσα), the lyre on which Polycrates made music, the ship's anchor Seleucus had had engraved, and a fisherman will remember the apostle and the children drawn out of the water [= the net]" (*Paed.*, III, 11, 59, 1). It is noteworthy that Clement includes among pagan symbols those which were already in use among Judaic Christians.

Justin also knew Noah's ark as a symbol of salvation. He enlarges on it in a remarkable passage of the *Dialogue with Trypho*: "The righteous Noah with the other people of the Flood, namely his wife, their three sons and their sons' wives, added up to the number eight and afforded the symbol of that day, eighth in number but first in power, on which Christ rose from the dead. Now Christ, 'the firstborn of every creature', has become in a new

[11] H. Leclercq, art. Navire in *D.A.C.L.*, XII, cols. 1008–21.

sense the head of another race, of those whom he has brought to a new birth, by water, faith and the wood which holds the mysteries of the cross, just as Noah was saved in the wood of the ark, floating on the waters with his family" (CXXXVIII, 1-2). In this conclusive passage the ark is the means of salvation. But what Justin is looking at is the wood of which the ark was made, as symbolizing the cross. This is certainly the only meaning presented by the salvation symbolism of the ark before Tertullian. On this point Goldammer is right, as against Peterson.

It remains for us to return to our starting-point and to ask at what moment we can detect a change in the symbolic use of the ship. When did its symbolism change from that of the cross to that of the Church? There are two lines of evidence of nearly the same date, which seem independent of one another. On the one hand, Tertullian in *De baptismo* is the first to make the ship an explicit symbol of the Church, with reference to the calming of the tempest. He rejects the baptismal interpretation, and goes on: "The ship prefigured the Church, which on the sea of this world is buffeted by the waves of persecution and temptation, while the Lord in his patience seems to sleep; till the last moment when, awakened by the prayer of the saints, he subdued the world and gives back peace to his own" (XII, 7).

The interest of this text is that it takes us right back to the beginning of the Church symbolism of the ship. Its continuity with the Jewish theme of deliverance is unquestionable. Peterson was right to emphasize the place it gives to the intercession of the saints and its eschatological character. We are very close to the Christian *Testament of Nephtali*. The calming of the tempest is its context. And the theme of the Church is but lightly touched. Notice that it is a question of the universal Church: the saints are the twelve apostles. This again is right in line with the ship carrying the twelve patriarchs, in the *Testaments*; so there is no doubt that we have here a development of the Judaeo-Christian theme. And, too, Tertullian opposes his exegesis to another, which sees the calming of the storm as a figure of baptism. We may well suppose that in this other exegesis the ship signified the cross, as in Justin's exegesis of Noah's ark. So there is a conflict between the two Judaeo-Christian lines we have encountered, one eschatological, in the *Testaments*, the other baptismal, in Justin.

But in any case Tertullian marks a decisive stage by his affirmation that the ship represents the Church. In *De idololatria* he repeats his statement, still more clearly, with reference to Noah's ark: "*Quod in arca non fuit, in Ecclesia non sit*" (24, 4). The same theme will appear in Cyprian's *De unitate Ecclesiae* and in Origen. It is the origin of the aphorism: "There is no salvation outside the Church." Emphasis is put on the unity of the Church and the necessity of belonging to her in order to be saved. Here there appears for the first time the symbolism of the Church as representing the necessary means of salvation. The expression will be taken up by Pope Callistus I, quoted by Hippolytus (*Elench.*, IX, 12, 23), and we find ourselves in the line of a Roman theology of Church unity.

But the catechetical developments we quoted at the beginning are not strictly reducible to this type. They show us the ship as an image of the local church and its structure. Now, we find this theme in texts of Hippolytus of Rome which so far we have not used. For example, in the *Benedictions of Moses*: "The ships are the churches, which are tossed about by the violence and roughness of the alien spirit of this world, and take refuge in the Lord as in a sheltered harbour" (*P.O.*, 27, p. 176). Hippolytus is the first writer to give us the catechetical allegory of the Church. Through his *Apostolic Tradition*, he is not unconnected with the sources of the *Apostolic Constitutions*. We are, therefore, moved to connect Hippolytus with the allegory of the local church which we met at the beginning of this inquiry, starting from ships as symbols of the churches.

Thus it appears that Tertullian and Hippolytus, independently of one another, were at the source of those developments which led to the ship being looked on as a symbol of the Church, whether the universal or the local church. In the case of both writers this symbolism has Judaeo-Christian roots, and would appear to have a special connection with the apocalyptic theme of the ship as a figure of Israel in the *Testaments of the Twelve Patriarchs*. This dependence is the more convincing where Hippolytus is concerned because he makes use of the *Testaments* elsewhere. This evolution was no doubt made easier by the place held in Hellenistic literature by the theme of the ship as symbol of the State. So we have one more example of the adaptation of a Judaeo-Christian image to a Hellenistic usage.

5

Elias's Chariot

Writers of the fourth century have left us some lists of
names for the sacrament of baptism which are valuable for
the light they throw on its various aspects. Cyril of Jerusalem, for instance, calls it "ransoming of prisoners,
forgiveness of sins, . . . rebirth of the soul, shining vesture
(ἔνδυμα), ineffaceable seal (σφραγίς), vehicle (ὄχημα) to
Heaven, delights of Paradise, pledge of kingship, gift of
adoption" (*Procatech.*, 16; *P.G.*, 33, 360A–361A). The same
list, with only verbal changes, is found in the *Homily on
Baptism* which is probably St Basil's (5; *P.G.*, 31, 433A).
Gregory Nazianzen gives two lists, one after the other.
The first includes "vehicle (ὄχημα) to God, pillar of faith,
perfection of the spirit, key to the kingdom of Heaven"
(*Or.*, XL, 3; *P.G.*, 36, 361B); the second lists "grace,
baptism, anointing (χρῖσμα), enlightenment, imperishable
vesture (ἔνδυμα), laver of regeneration, seal (σφραγίς)"
(4; 361C).

These are traditional titles, and I have studied several of
them elsewhere. Some of them are familiar to us. But
one, occurring in all three lists, is very peculiar, namely,
"vehicle", ὄχημα. Is it possible to decide what image it
alludes to, and consequently which aspect of baptism it
emphasizes? On the other hand, can its origin in tradition
be determined? I propose to devote this study to the
elucidation of this point of ancient baptismal catechesis.
It will be of interest in confronting us with an expression
which belongs both to philosophical and to religious

language, and we shall see that in reality two very different lines of thought are involved.

The word ὄχημα, which in its proper sense designates any sort of vehicle, was used with a clearly defined meaning in the philosophical language of the fourth and fifth centuries B.C., and this is the sense we shall consider first. It meant the body considered as the vehicle of the soul. This use of the word goes back to Plato's *Timaeus*, where we read: "The gods have given the whole body as the vehicle (ὄχημα) of the soul" (69C). This sense is common in Middle Platonism. J. H. Waszink has noted several examples:[1] Albinus, for instance, says that the gods have placed the body beneath the soul to serve as vehicle for it (XXIII, 1). Maximus of Tyre speaks of "the blessed soul which remembers the God who has put it on the vehicle (ὄχημα) and ordained it to be its driver" (*Disc.*, XLI, 4).[2]

The same meaning is found in Christian writers, such as Clement of Alexandria (*Strom.*, VI, 18, 163, 2) and Methodius of Olympus (*Res.*, II, 22; *G.C.S.*, p. 376). Gregory of Nyssa asks what becomes of the soul after death when its vehicle has fallen to pieces (*De an. et res.*; *P.G.*, 46, 45B). The continuation of this passage seems to show that the image Gregory has in mind is that of a ship, with the soul as pilot, not as driver. The word ὄχημα can of course be applied to a ship as well as a carriage, but Gregory knows the sense of carriage too (*Ep.* 1; *P.G.*, 46, 1001B: *Ep.*, 2; *P.G.*, 1013B). Plato seems to have thought mostly in the latter sense when comparing the body to a vehicle. Tertullian translates ὄχημα by *vectaculum* to indicate the

---

[1] *Tertulliani De anima* (Amsterdam, 1947), p. 542.
[2] See also *Hermès Trismégiste*, X, 13, with Festugière's note, pp. 128–9; Pseudo-Plutarch, *Vita Hom.*, 122.

body (*Anim.*, 53, 3), St Augustine by *vehiculum* (*Epist.*, 13, 2).

In this sense the image of the ὄχημα has been integrated into a common philosophical tradition, of Platonic type but in an elementary form. But in Neoplatonism we meet a more technical conception, in which ὄχημα does not designate the terrestrial body, but the astral bodies which the soul puts on successively in the course of its ascent through the planetary spheres.[3] This teaching is particularly developed by Proclus,[4] in whom, as Jean Trouillard has shown,[5] it signifies that there is a fundamental corporeity, but that it is "the point of insertion for supplementary casings". In his *Commentary on the Timaeus*, Proclus specifies that the νοῦς is carried by the ψυχή, that the ψυχή in its turn has a vehicle of fire (αἰθέριον ὄχημα), and lastly that there is a terrestrial body (γήινον σῶμα) (I, p. 5; II ff. Diehl).

This conception gives a synthetic picture of several lines of thought, all of which go back to Plato. The doctrine of the soul as vehicle of the νοῦς comes from the *Phaedrus* (246A), where the word ὄχημα does not appear, but where the chariot drawn by winged horses is the vehicle of the νοῦς. Methodius of Olympus uses ὄχημα in a passage which explicitly refers to this context: "There is need for strong, generous natures which, floating straight forward on the tide of sensibility, conduct the chariot (ὄχημα) of the soul to the heights; until, never swerving from their course but mounting nimbly (κούφως) beyond the world through the

---

[3] See G. Verbecke, *L'Évolution de la doctrine du pneuma, du stoïcisme à saint Augustin* (Paris, 1945), pp. 363–79; J. J. Poortman, *Ochêma* (Assen, 1954).

[4] *Elements of Theology*, pp. 207–10. See notes by E. R. Dodds, pp. 304–9, 313–21.

[5] "Réflexions sur l'ὄχημα dans Proclus", in *R.E.G.*, 70 (1957), pp. 103–7.

sharp quickness of the mind, they settle upon the canopy
(ἁψίς) of heaven and contemplate unchangingness without
distraction" (*Conv.*, I, 1; *G.C.S.*, pp. 7–8). Here the whole
vocabulary has reference to the Phaedrus myth.

At the other extreme we meet the theme of the terrestrial body with which we started. But between the two
comes the characteristically Neoplatonic notion, for
which Proclus reserves the name of ὄχημα, that of the astral
body, intermediate between the earthly body and the soul.
This conception also originates with Plato. In the *Timaeus*
(41DE), speaking of the first creation of souls by the
Demiurge, he shows us the Demiurge "dividing souls
into a number equal to that of the stars, allotting one soul
to each star and making it board its star as if it were a
chariot (ὄχημα), in order to enable it to see the nature of
the universe". Thus the first body given to souls is a
vehicle made of fire; only later do they receive the
terrestrial vehicle (44E). This conception persisted in
Platonism, before Neoplatonism. We meet it in Origen
particularly, and Methodius of Olympus reproaches him
for it: "He says that, after going forth from this world,
the soul has another vehicle (ὄχημα), analogous in form to
the sensible vehicle. This is to declare that the soul is
incorporeal, in the Platonist manner. To say that after
having left this world the soul needs a vehicle and a vesture
(περιβολή), as not being able to subsist in nakedness, what is
this but to say it is incorporeal?" (*Res.*, III, 18; *G.C.S.*,
pp. 414–15).[6]

Origen's thesis is that the soul is wholly incorporeal,
clothing itself in various bodies. This was the thesis of
Plotinus a little later. It is possible that Origen and

---

[6] See J. Daniélou, "La Résurrection des corps chez Grégoire de Nysse",
in *V.C.*, 7 (1953), pp. 166–70.

Plotinus may have taken it from the same source, perhaps Ammonius Saccas. The thesis was to be modified by Proclus, who admits that the soul always keeps a certain corporeity, as Trouillard observes (*op. cit.*, p. 104). But from the point of view that we are concerned with, the interesting thing is the doctrine, common in this age, of the astral body. Before the discussions of the Neoplatonists, this doctrine was held in one current of Middle Platonism. It is found in Origen, and he certainly got it from Middle Platonism. A passage in the *Hermetic Books*, speaking of the way in which the soul is carried (ὀχεῖται), explains, in a way that foreshadows Proclus, that the soul is the vehicle of the λόγος, the λόγος of the πνεῦμα (which is connected with our ὄχημα), and the πνεῦμα of the earthly body (x, 13).

There is one more thing to be noticed. For Neoplatonism, this astral body, which comes from the ether, is what enables the soul, in itself motionless, to move. J. Bidez points this out with reference to Porphyry.[7] Iamblichus makes several allusions to the idea: "Souls of differing kinds connote their vehicles (ὀχήματα) in accordance with the rank assigned to each" (379, 25; Festugière, p. 221). This is a direct echo from the *Timaeus*, 41E. Later on Iamblichus says: "Certain Platonists believe that between the incorporeal soul and the corporeal vessel (ἀγγεῖον) there are ethereal, heavenly and spiritual garments, which serve the soul as vehicles" (385, 4–8; Festugière, p. 237).[8] Souls therefore move on these fiery vehicles. Does the

[7] *Vie de Porphyre* (Ghent, 1913), pp. 89–90B. See also J. Pépin, "Le Symbolisme néo-platonicien de la vêture", in *Augustinus Magister*, I, p. 298.

[8] See also Julian, *Disc.*, IV, 152B; Hertlein, p. 197: the Sun gives something of the divine light as a vehicle for a secure descent into the world of becoming. J. Pépin quotes this text (*op. cit.*, p. 298), but interprets it wrongly.

astral body assimilated to these vehicles give us the origin of the baptismal use of the word?

Certain elements might incline us to think so, in particular the association with ἔνδυμα, current in Neoplatonism. It would then be a matter, not of a fiery body superseding the earthly body, but of the divine πνεῦμα vivifying the whole man, body and soul. To this would be added the idea of quickening's being at the same time a carrying up of the baptized person into the heavenly sphere, not of the stars but of the Godhead himself. We have noticed elsewhere that a parallel image, also borrowed from Plato, is used in this sense by the Fathers; the wings which raise the soul to the height of Heaven become the wings of that dove, the Holy Spirit, who raises the soul to the Trinity.[9]

Nevertheless, research into the symbolism of the ὄχημα amongst the Fathers of the Church shows another line, deriving from the Bible. There are several relevant passages, of which the first is Ezechiel 1. 4 ff., the vision of God borne up by the seraphim. These are assimilated to wheels, and so it is God's chariot, the *merkabah*, that is meant. This is called ὄχημα in Old Testament apocrypha (*Test. Abr.*, 10) and the word is repeated by the fourth-century Fathers. Thus we read in Gregory Nazianzen: "Ezechiel describes God's vehicle (ὄχημα), that is the cherubim, and the throne which is above them and the firmament above the throne and him who is described as in the firmament" (*Or.*, 28, 19; *P.G.*, 36, 52A). In the Septuagint *merkabah* is translated by ἅρμα (Ez. 43. 3), but Gregory is more exact in using ὄχημα, of which the sense is more general.

[9] See J. Daniélou, "La colombe et la ténèbre", in *Eranos Jahrbuch*, 23 (1955), pp. 389-418.

Before the fourth century, the same translation is found in a notable passage of Methodius of Olympus. He is criticizing Origen's spiritual ὄχημα, and sets out to show that the body is always composed of four elements. For that purpose he uses the analogy of the microcosm and the macrocosm: the world as a whole is composed of the four elements, and so too is the human body. He goes on: "That is why the prophet [Ezechiel], wanting to show God's presidency and governance of the universe,... expounds the guidance (ἡνιόχησις) and intelligent management of the four-faced cherubim as directed by the Logos.... Man, being a heavenly plant, corresponds exactly to air; because of his speed, the lion symbolizes fire; the ox symbolizes earth, and the eagle water, because birds are born from water. God, then,... holding air and earth, water and fire in his hand and ruling them by his will, like a four-horsed vehicle (ὄχημα), in an unutterable way controls (ἡνιοχεῖ) the universe and keeps it in being" (*Res.*, II, 10; *G.C.S.*, pp. 351–2).

We see that Methodius here assimilates the *merkabah* to Hellenistic ideas. The *Cohortatio* of Pseudo-Justin had already likened it to the winged chariot of Zeus in the *Phaedrus*, 246E. But there is an allusion to a more philosophical notion, that of the cosmic chariot. It is in the *Treatise on the World*, which belongs to the first century of our era and represents a neo-Aristotelian conception (400B; Festugière, *Le Dieu cosmique*, p. 475). Again, it is explicitly developed, with the theme of the four elements, in a text of Dion Chrysostom, which seems to have some Iranian features.[10]

These interpretations were soon taken up into biblical

---

[10] J. Bidez, *Les Mages hellénisés*, II (Paris, 1938), pp. 142–3; F. Buffière, *Les Mythes d'Homère et la pensée grecque* (Paris, 1956), pp. 113–14.

exegesis. Philo compares the four animals of Genesis 15. 9 to the four elements (*Quaest. Gen.*, III, 3). Closer to Methodius is Irenaeus, who interprets the four animals of Ezechiel as the four cardinal points, giving them a cosmic significance (*Adv. haer.*, III, 11, 8). We shall come across these assimilations again; what matters at the moment is Methodius's use of the term ὄχημα for the *merkabah*.

Is there reason to think that this theme had a relation to baptism? A curious passage in Tertullian's *De baptismo* shows us in the primordial waters "the vehicle (*vectaculum*) of God". As Waszink notes, the word is the exact translation of ὄχημα. It is a neologism of Tertullian. In all likelihood the theme of the *merkabah* underlies it, and probably R. F. Refoulé is right in translating it "throne". Indeed, when eulogizing water, Tertullian seeks to show that there was a time when it was the only element, and therefore the *merkabah*. Moreover, Cyril of Jerusalem, in a baptismal context, speaks of Christ walking on the water as "the charioteer (ἡνίοχος) of the sea" (*Paral.*, 8; *P.G.*, 33, 1140B), and as "the charioteer and creator (ποιητής) of the waters" (*ibid.*, 9; 1141A). The word "charioteer" here calls up the image of Neptune driving his chariot and horses, which are the sea itself. But the expression "driver and creator" enlarges the image of the sense of the cosmic chariot, and so joins up with Dion Chrysostom and Methodius.

A second biblical theme to be taken into consideration is the chariot that bore Elias to Heaven. The text is quoted by the fourth-century Fathers. In the same passage where he mentions the *merkabah*, Gregory Nazianzen says: "A chariot (ἅρμα) of fire takes Elias up to Heaven (πρὸς οὐρανόν), showing that the just person is above man"

(*Or.* 28, 19; *P.G.*, 36, 49C). Gregory of Nyssa often
alludes to it: "Like Elias, our mind (διάνοια) is taken up in
the chariot of fire and carried through the air to the glories
of Heaven—by fire we may understand the Holy Spirit"
(*In Cant.*, 10; *P.G.*, 44, 980C. See *Beat.*, 6; 1272D; *Laud.
Basil.*; *P.G.*, 46, 804C). These texts relate to spiritual
ascension. Another passage sees Elias's chariot as a figure
of the Incarnation: it represents the divine nature which
came down to earth and afterwards went up again, carrying
human nature into Heaven. Cyril of Jerusalem also associates the chariot of Elias with Christ's ascension (*Cat.*,
XIV, 25; *P.G.*, 33, 857B).

The fact that the word ἅρμα is ordinarily used presents
a difficulty in connecting Elias's chariot with the theme of
the baptismal vehicle. But ὄχημα is found sometimes, as in
the Macarian *Homilies*, XXV, 9 (*P.G.*, 34, 673B), and one
may ask whether certain texts do not give ὄχημα in a
context referring to Elias's chariot. There is here a passage
in Gregory of Nyssa which has considerable analogies
with that from the commentary on the Canticle: "How
can anyone reach the heights if he be engrossed in the
things of earth? How will he wing his way (ἀναπτείη)
towards Heaven if he be not borne by the celestial wing
(πτερῷ) . . . ? Who is so ignorant of the evangelical
mysteries that he does not know that there is but one
vehicle (ὄχημα) for the journey to the Heavens, which is
to be likened to the form of the dove in flight whose wings
the prophet David longed to have? It is in this way that
Scripture is wont to symbolize the power of the Spirit"
(*Virg.*, 11; *P.G.*, 46, 365BC).

Here Gregory seems to join two distinct themes. On
the one hand there is that of wings, which comes from
Plato's *Phaedrus*; but that of the ὄχημα appears to be

different. Wings and vehicle are both images of the power of the Holy Spirit. Further back we have found Gregory assimilating Elias's chariot to the power of the Spirit; it seems probable that it is to this chariot he now alludes by the word ὄχημα. The parallelism of the wing and the ὄχημα appears in other places in Gregory's works; for instance, in the first *Treatise on the Psalms*, 5: "The glory of God is like a vehicle (ὄχημα) and a wing (πτερόν) to him who is gripped by God's hand, when he turns his back on shameful deeds" (*P.G.*, 44, 456A). The hand of God is one of the names of the Holy Spirit; here again it is he who is the vehicle which raises the soul.[11]

So it seems possible that the ὄχημα πρὸς οὐρανόν, which denotes baptism in Cyril of Jerusalem, Gregory Nazianzen and Basil, is a reference to the chariot of Elias. But have we reason to think that that chariot was brought into relation with baptism? That is precisely the case for two of those writers. There is an important text in which Cyril treats the taking-up of Elias as a figure of baptism: "Elias is taken up, but through water: first he crosses the Jordan, then horses carry him (ἱππηλατεῖ) to Heaven" (*Cat.*, 3, 6; *P.G.*, 33, 433A). The image is plain: it shows baptism effected by cleansing in water (symbolized by the crossing of Jordan) together with the rising to Heaven which denotes the giving of the Spirit.

The connection between Elias's ascension and the Jordan must be noticed; it has contributed to the bringing together of his chariot with baptism. The connection is biblical, and is emphasized by the eschatological tradition in particular. The theme of Elias's ascension, without being frequent, is well attested, and that of the Jordan is associated with it. It is possible that it is represented on a

[11] See also the expression βασιλείας ὄχημα (*Asc. Chr.*; *P.G.*, 46, 692CD).

fresco in the cemetery of Domitilla (*D.A.C.L.*, IV, 2671). In any case it appears on sarcophagi, either in the form of waves representing water or of a person lying beneath the chariot, in the way the ancients represented rivers.[12] This iconological association of Jordan, always connected with baptism, with the ascension of Elias could not but lead to seeing in the latter a figure of baptism.

In the same sermon in which he calls baptism ὄχημα πρὸς θεόν, Gregory Nazianzen explains the association of Elias's chariot with baptismal grace. Commenting on the designation of baptism as φώτισμα, he mentions a number of Old-Testament events in which there was an appearing of light: "It was light which carried off Elias in the fiery chariot (ἅρμα), carried him off without consuming him. . . . Most especially, light is the baptismal irradiation which contains the great and wondrous mystery of our salvation" (*Or.*, 40, 6; *P.G.*, 36, 365AB). Again light is a symbol of the power of the Holy Spirit. It is the fieriness of Elias's chariot that is considered here, rather than its being a vehicle to Heaven. But it is still the same context, in which baptismal grace is signified in its aspect of power of the Holy Spirit which carries one away into the life of Heaven.[13]

So the context to which the baptismal symbolism of the ὄχημα is referred appears principally to be the carrying-away of Elias. We say "principally", because the Fathers draw analogies between the *merkabah* of Ezechiel, Elias's chariot, and yet other figures. There is an example in Gregory of Nyssa which is specially interesting on account

[12] H. Leclercq, *D.A.C.L.*, art. Helios, VI, 2148–51.
[13] See also St Ambrose: "Elias unclosed Heaven, and was carried thither by the chariot; you too can go up there if you receive the sacrament of grace" (*De Helia et jejunio*, 22, 85; *C.S.E.L.*, p. 464).

7+

of its baptismal context. It refers to the passage of the Red Sea and the chariots of the Egyptians and of the Israelites: "There was an unconquerable force (δύναμις) bringing destruction on the Egyptians through the marvels concerning the sea, a force that the Scriptures call horsemen. . . . But David makes mention also of God's chariot (ἅρμα) when he writes: 'The chariot of God is more than tens of thousands', including in the number the thousands of drivers. And, too, the Scriptures give the name 'horses' to the power (δύναμις) which raised the prophet Elias from earth to the ethereal region" (*In Cant.*, 3; *P.G.*, 44, 812AB). Baptism imparts to the baptized this δύναμις which the chariot symbolizes: "It is not possible to be made like to the horsemen which submerged the chariots of the Egyptians in the deep if one has not been freed from slavery to the Enemy by the sacramental water" (813A). Here the *merkabah* and Elias's chariot and the chariots of Israel are parallel symbols of the grace of the Spirit given when the baptismal Jordan has been crossed.

There is, possibly, one last biblical context which points in a different direction and to another *milieu*. The 38th *Ode of Solomon* begins in this way: "I went up to the light of truth as if into a chariot (*markabhta*): and the Truth took me and led me . . . and from the rocks and the waves it preserved me" (1–2). The word *markabhta* denotes any kind of vehicle. It is the Syriac equivalent to *merkabah*, and it could mean a chariot. But, as J. H. Bernard has rightly pointed out,[14] the context indicates something else. The waves mentioned in verse 2 suggest a voyage, and the Syriac word could perfectly well have this sense; so could the Greek ὄχημα, which is the exact translation. We have here, then, an ὄχημα which is a ship. We know

[14] *The Odes of Solomon* (Cambridge, 1912), p. 123.

that the context of the *Odes* is baptismal, and accordingly ὄχημα appears here as a name for baptism.[15] This indication is the more valuable in that the *Odes of Solomon* go back to the second century and an archaic Judaeo-Christian context.

We have seen that the ship had a biblical reference. J. H. Bernard seems again to be right when he thinks of the Flood, a *locus classicus* of baptismal typology. In it, the ark has a place of the first importance. In Justin, the ark denotes the δύναμις of Christ which is at work in water (*Dial.*, cxxxviii, 2–3); this is found again in Cyril of Jerusalem (*Cat.*, 17, 10; *P.G.*, 33, 982A). Tertullian saw it as a figure of the Church (*De idol.*, 24), and this was to persist in the West. But in *Ode 38* the ὄχημα denotes the idea of the divine δύναμις. This is very close to the ideas we have met concerning Elias's chariot. The allusion to the Flood is confirmed by a text of Ephraem, wherein Noah's ark is called "vehicle" (*r'khubheh*) in a baptismal context. But this depends on another theme, that of the symbolism of the ship.

Our biblical inquiry leads to the practical recognition of two scriptural origins of ὄχημα applied to baptism. On the one hand, we find the term translating *merkabah*, the vehicle of Yahweh in Ezechiel, but without clear reference to our theme. On the other hand, the baptismal theme appears in connection with the ascension of Elias, though the prophet's chariot is rarely called ὄχημα. It therefore seems that the baptismal ὄχημα is a result of the fusion of the two themes. Is it possible to find a context which explains this fourth-century fusion? That their connection

[15] J. Daniélou, *The Bible and the Liturgy* (Notre Dame, Indiana, 1956). (French text, 2nd ed. [Paris, 1951], pp. 304–18).

was normal we have learned from Gregory of Nyssa. But can it be shown how it came about that baptism was looked on as representing the Christian's ascent on God's vehicle?

Let us say in the first place that the idea does not look impossible. Indeed, it can be found in St John Chrysostom, in an eschatological context. When commenting on I Thessalonians 4. 17, he compares the ἀπάντησις of an earthly king or of an affectionate father with that when the blessed will go on the clouds to meet Christ; and he writes: "His children, and those who are worthy to be his children, set forth on a vehicle (ὄχημα) to see and greet him . . . ; we are carried on the vehicle of the Father. For he received him in the clouds, and we shall be caught up in the clouds" (*Hom.*, 8; *P.G.*, 62, 440). There is here a comparison between Christ's ascension and that of the Christian: the one was on the *merkabah* and thus will it be with the other. Observe this linking of the *merkabah* with Christ's ascension: it reminds us of the old Antiochene tradition, that of the *Gospel of Peter*, xxx and the *Ascension of Isaias*, II, 17.

But the interesting thing is that Chrysostom thinks it natural that Christians, in their final ascent to Heaven, should also be carried on the *merkabah*, the ὄχημα τοῦ Πατρός. To explain this point it seems we should have again to turn to Hellenistic representations. The philosophical theme of the ὄχημα comes first to mind; however, we are not concerned with that here, but rather with another, more mythological, line, that of apotheosis conceived as a carrying-off in the chariot of Helios.

F. Cumont has studied the origins of this imagery,[16] which is doubtless of Eastern origin. It is found associated

[16] *Lux perpetua* (Paris, 1949), pp. 289–93.

with Mithraism. It first appears applied to emperors, in connection with the solar cult. Thus his Latin panegyrist writes of Constantius: "You whom the sun itself welcomes to its chariot to carry you above" (*Panegyric*, VI, 14) Or again, Eunapius quotes an oracle informing Julian that after his death he will be carried up by the vehicle (ὄχημα) of the sun: "Then a vehicle of dazzling flame (περιλαμπὲς ὄχημα) will bear you to Olympus; and you will reach the paternal abode in ethereal light" (Frag. 26; *F.H.G.*, IV, 24–5). From the beginning of the empire pictorial representations depict emperors carried away in a chariot drawn by winged horses (Cumont, *op. cit.*, p. 293); and this honour was accorded also to less distinguished persons.

There is evidence for such representations being adopted both by Jews and Christians. For the Jews, there are several examples of the chariot of Helios in the Galilean synagogues. Thus, at Beth Alpha, Helios in his chariot drawn by four horses abreast is surrounded by the signs of the Zodiac and of the seasons. The same is found at Naaran and Isfija. These motifs are sometimes regarded simply as decoration; but Goodenough considers that they have a mystical and eschatological significance, as symbolical of the soul's ascent to God. This view seems especially justified at the Naaran synagogue, where the theme is associated with the deliverance of Daniel.[17] A mosaic in the synagogue at Hamman Lif in Tunisia shows a wheel among other salvation themes. Goodenough thinks that this may be "shorthand" for the chariot of God as the conveyance of souls to Heaven.

Similarly in ancient Christian art. A fresco in the catacomb of SS. Peter and Marcellinus shows the sun in a chariot

[17] Goodenough, *Jewish Symbols*, I, pp. 248, 250–1, 255–6, 258.

drawn by two horses.[18] But more particularly must be mentioned the mosaic in the little Christian subterranean chamber (hypogeum) discovered on the Vatican. It represents the chariot of Helios, and interpretations of it aver that it is an allusion to Christ as "Sun of justice". But is this a sufficient explanation? The other mosaics in the hypogeum depict the classical scenes of deliverance which refer both to baptism and resurrection—Jonah, the Good Shepherd carrying the sheep, the Fisherman and fish. One can hardly fail to associate the chariot of Christ-Helios with the same group and to see in it the expression of Christian eschatological hope.[19] So we are back at Goodenough's interpretation of the same scene in the synagogue, with the difference that now it is Christ who is represented under the features of Helios.

The presence of the chariot of Helios in Christian art, with its eschatological significance, is therefore well attested. But is this purely and simply a borrowing from pagan mythology? The parallel examples of the Good Shepherd and the Fisherman, whose style is taken from Hellenistic art but which are referred to biblical topics, suggest that it is the same here. In fact, archaeological as well as literary research shows that there is such biblical reference, and it is precisely to the chariot of Elias. Dom Leclercq has rightly drawn attention to the strict parallelism between representations of Elias going up in his chariot and the chariot of Helios. All the evidence goes to show that the representation of Elias's chariot was suggested by classical representations of that of Helios (*D.A.C.L.*, VI, 2147–9).

[18] J. Wilpert, *Le Pitture delle catacumbe romane*, pl. cix, n. 2.

[19] See also fragment 6 of Melito, in which Christ's baptism in the Jordan is associated with the sun's bath in the ocean. On this text see R. M. Grant, "Melito of Sardis on Baptism", in *V.C.*, 4 (1950), pp. 33–6.

There is literary confirmation of this assimilation in texts which, playing on the Greek names Ἠλιάς and Ἥλιος, compare the prophet with the sun. This is implied in a text of Chrysostom, who writes of Elias: "Then and now he shines more brightly than the sun, his glory is spread over all the earth on which the sun looks down" (*Hom. Eliam*, I, 3; *P.G.*, 63, 464). Sedulius mentions the likeness between the two names explicitly: "Elias, shining in name and in merit, is worthy to shed his light on the pathways of Heaven: by the change of one letter his name in Greek becomes 'sun'" (I, 186). This resemblance of names is carried over to an analogy of images and implies that the figure of Elias was associated with solar images.

So then, the patristic theme of the ὄχημα is seen to be in the first place a gathering together of several biblical images of celestial vehicles, essentially the *merkabah* of Ezechiel and Elias's chariot. In addition, Christians came to give it importance at the archaeological level because of the big part played by the chariot of Helios in Hellenic symbolism of the soul's celestial journey. But in taking over Hellenistic images, Christians kept the biblical idea. There is a parallel to this in the case of wings. These come from the imagery in the *Phaedrus*, but for Christians they denote the wings of the dove, the Holy Spirit. In the same way the ὄχημα took elements from representations of the sun-chariot: but it too signifies the power of the Holy Spirit, who is ὄχημα and πτερόν.

Accordingly, we have an answer to the question we started with. The designation of baptism as ὄχημα πρὸς οὐρανόν has reference to a biblical theme, as have the other names for baptism. This theme combines the image of the *merkabah* with that of Elias's chariot. Its popularity was no doubt facilitated by its analogy with the theme of the sun-chariot. But its content is essentially to denote baptism as the action of the Holy Spirit raising the soul from earthly life to heavenly life. Thus it points to an essential aspect of baptism, just as σφραγίς, ἔνδυμα, βάπτισμα, χρῖσμα, φωτισμός point to other aspects of it.

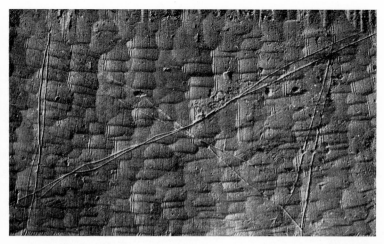

1. Axe scratched on the side of a stone ossuary from the cemetery of Dominus Flevit, Mount Olivet, Jerusalem (*photo: Laboratorio di Terra Santa*)

2. Cross in the form of an axe engraved on a stone found near the Great Theatre, Ephesus

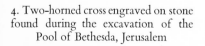

3. Six-pointed cross or star incised on the cover of a stone ossuary in the Department of Antiquities of Jordan

4. Two-horned cross engraved on stone found during the excavation of the Pool of Bethesda, Jerusalem

5 & 6. Ploughs scratched on ossuaries from the cemetery of Dominus Flevit. This type of plough is still in use in the Near East. In 6 the head of the plough has been depicted as raised to make the cross symbolism clear

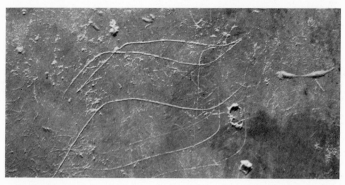

7. The fish was a common symbol among the Judeo-Christians. This graffito from the Dominus Flevit cemetery shows a whale (?) in the sea

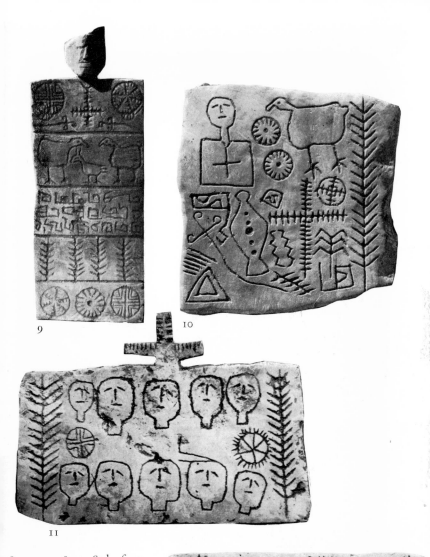

9   10

11

8, 9, 10, 11 & 12. Stelae from the cemetery discovered at Khirbet Kilkis, near Hebron. They belong to a fourth-century heretical gnostic sect, the Archontici. Symbols shown include notched crosses, sword crosses, Tree of Life, stars, chariot wheels, palm branches and the *lulab*. The birds have been interpreted as phoenixes symbolizing resurrection

12

13. Part of the inscriptions in the tomb of Nur at Bethphage. They relate to the millenarian beliefs common among early Christians (cf. Apoc. 20. 1–5). *Left to right:* the sign for 1000, palm branch or Tree of Life linked with millenarian themes in the Old Testament, the harp of David to attract souls to the Kingdom of Heaven. The Greek letters, like those of the Hebrew alphabet, have each a complex symbolic meaning (*photo: P. S. Voigt*)

14. Cross combined with Tree of Life or palm branch. Part of fourth-century mosaic floor of chapel at Beth ha-Shitta

15. Tree of Life, the middle one as a cross, incised on the end of an ossuary from Dominus Flevit cemetery

6

The Plough and the Axe

Among the texts from Isaias included in the collection of
Testimonia are verses 3 and 4 of chapter 2: "For the Law
shall come forth from Sion, and the word of the Lord from
Jerusalem . . . . They shall turn their swords into ploughshares and their spears into sickles. Nation shall not lift
up sword against nation, neither shall they be exercised
any more to war." Justin quotes this text more than
once;[1] Cyprian mentions it in his *Testimonia*;[2] it is found
in Origen's *Against Celsus*.[3] It would be interesting to
write the story of its interpretation. The earliest authors
understand it as referring to the forgiveness of offences and
the non-violence that characterize the Church; from
Eusebius on, it is applied to the Peace of Constantine and
the political unity of the world.[4]

Irenaeus has occasion to mention this text in his treatise
Against Heresies, and he begins by explaining it in the
general sense of the peaceful Christian spirit, in accordance
with the old exegesis: "The law of liberty, that is, God's
word proclaimed throughout the earth by the apostles,
who came from Jerusalem, has wrought a great change.
The swords and spears of warfare are turned into tools of
peace, into ploughs that he himself has made, into sickles
that he has provided for the harvest: so much so that men
no longer think of fighting, but turn the other cheek when

[1] *Apol.*, XXXIX, 1; *Dial.*, CX, 3.
[2] *Test.*, II, 18; *C.S.E.L.*, 84–5.
[3] *Contra Cels.*, V, 33; *G.C.S.*, pp. 35–6.
[4] *Dem. ev.*, 9; *P.G.*, 22, 712C–D.

they are struck. He who has done these things is the one of whom the prophets spoke, of him and no other. It is indeed our Lord—and in this the saying is true" (IV, 34, 4). This exegesis is very close to that of Justin, and calls for no special remark.

But Irenaeus goes on to develop this prophetical interpretation into a very subtle allegory, as he sometimes does: "For it is our Lord himself who has made the plough and provided the sickle: this signifies the first seed-time of man, who was patterned in Adam, and the gathering of the harvest by the Word at the end of time. And consequently, he who joined the beginning with the end, and is the Lord of both, has finally shown forth the plough, wood combined with iron, and so has weeded his land: for the 'materialized' Word, made one with flesh and fixed in the way it has been, has cleared the untilled earth" (IV, 34, 4).

The beginning of this passage is clear. In the plough Irenaeus sees a symbol of the creation, of man's patterning, considered as a sowing; and in the sickle he sees a symbol of the last judgement, when the righteous will be harvested and housed in the barns of Heaven. It is obvious that the passage in St John's gospel about him who sows and him who reaps (4. 35 ff.) underlies the text; moreover, the words "in this the saying is true" are quoted from it. Irenaeus has twice commented on them a little before (IV, 23, 1; 25, 3). But Irenaeus does not stop there. The Word joins the beginning with the end (cf. III, 20, 4): that is to say that the plough which was at the beginning reappears at the end. Here we have Irenaeus's idea of "recapitulation", according to which Christ came to resume that which had been done in Adam: he who shaped man restores him at the last.

It is here that Irenaeus develops the symbolism of the plough. He takes up several aspects of it: "wood combined with iron", the "fixing" of the wood, the uprooting of weeds. This is the symbol we seek to clarify.

Irenaeus explicitly formulates certain of its elements. The first is the union of wood and iron in the plough. He sees in this a symbol of the union of the divine and human natures in Christ: "The Lord . . . has finally shown forth the plough, wood combined with iron, and so has weeded his land: for the 'materialized' (*firmum*) Word, made one with flesh and fixed in the way it has been, has cleared the untilled earth."

The parallelism between wood and iron, Word and flesh is clear enough. The order of the words might make us think that the wood signifies the Word, and the iron the human nature. But the epithet *firmum* applied to the Word, and the term *confixus*, suggest rather the iron of the plough. That this second interpretation is certainly the right one is guaranteed by another passage in Irenaeus. It is one referring to the incident in 4 [2] Kings 6. 5–7, where the axe belonging to the sons of the prophets falls into the Jordan, and Eliseus brings it to the surface by throwing a piece of wood into the water. This brings us to the axe, which also is made of wood and iron.

Now, Irenaeus comments on this passage thus: "The prophet showed that the 'materialized' (στερεόν) Logos of God, lost by us through neglect, had to be retrieved through the economy of the wood [of the cross] (ξύλον). John the Baptist says that the Word of God is like an axe (ἀξίνη); 'Now the axe is laid to the root of the tree'. . . . The economy of the wood has shown forth (ἐφανέρωσεν) this Word which was hidden from us" (v, 17, 4). This passage is clearly related to the one about the plough.

They have several phrases in common, which fortunately give us the Greek equivalents of the Latin text (στερεόν = *firmum*; ἐφανέρωσεν = *ostendit*). Here, iron is the divine nature, the Word, which was separated from human nature by sin and became hidden, and is brought to the surface, shown forth, by the Incarnation.

Irenaeus did not invent the symbolism of the prophet's axe: it is found in Justin, and this proves the great age of the symbol of iron joined to wood. But it must be observed that in Justin the iron signifies sinful man: the stress is not on the enduringness, the solidity, of iron, but on its heavy sluggishness. "Eliseus threw a piece of wood into the Jordan, and by doing so fished up the axe-head. . . . Just so, when we were sunk in the weighty sins we had committed, did our Christ ransom us through his crucifixion on the tree and by sanctifying us through [our baptism in] water" (*Dial.*, LXXXVI, 6). Justin's interpretation is found again in Tertullian: "What is more plain than this figure of wood? The hard-heartedness of this world, sunk in the deep waters of error, is freed by the wood of Christ, that is, by his passion" (*Adv. Jud.*, 13, 19; *P.L.*, 2, 676B).

In the fourth century the same interpretation is given by St Ambrose (*Sacram.*, II, 11; *S.C.*, p. 65: *Myst.*, 51; *S.C.*, p. 125).[5] But the most explicit author is Didymus: "The iron lost in the dark depths signifies man's nature, fallen from light. . . . The wood, taken and thrown in where the wanted object lies, symbolizes the glorious cross" (*Trin.*, II; *P.G.*, 39, 697C). This cannot be misunderstood: iron stands for human nature, weighed down by the burden of sin; wood is the wood of the cross. It is useful to recall

[5] See also Pseudo-Irenaeus, Frag. 26, 28, Harvey, II, 492–3; and Pseudo-Jerome, *Com. Marc.*, *P.L.* 30, 637C.

here that in early Christianity the cross was looked on as a symbol of divine power. This is apparent in the *Gospel of Peter* (41) and in the Christian *Sibylline Oracles* (VIII, ll. 217 ff.).[6] Justin speaks of the power (δύναμις) of the cross (*I Apol.*, XXXV, 2), and sees it as "the greatest sign of [Christ's] might and authority" (LV, 2).

Anyway, what matters for us is that the parallelism between the symbols of axe and plough justifies us in recognizing the wood of the plough as a symbol of the cross, since it is so for the wood of the axe. The plough, then, in so far as it is wood, is already a symbol of the cross. There is nothing surprising in that, when we remember the many places in the Old Testament where we come upon examples of ξύλον in which second-century writers saw symbols of the cross: the tree of Paradise, Moses' rod, the wood of the ark, and so forth.

But in the case of the plough—and doubtless of the axe too (*Adv. haer.*, V, 17, 4; *P.G.*, 7, 1471C)—there is something else, namely, its shape. Irenaeus writes: "The 'materialized' Word, made one with flesh and fixed as it has been (*habitu tali confixus*) ...". The way in which the Word is joined to the flesh thus resembles the way in which iron is fixed to the plough, the flesh being symbolized by the cross. Here the text is more difficult. The words *habitu tali* can be interpreted in several ways. And at first the image seems surprising. But here again we are faced with convergencies that make it difficult to question the interpretation we suggest.[7]

The plough as symbol of the cross occurs explicitly in Justin's *First Apology* (LV, 2–6). He sets down various

---

[6] J. Daniélou, *Théologie du judéo-christianisme*, pp. 294–303.

[7] See the objections of J. Doignon, "Le Salut par le fer et le bois chez saint Irénée", in *R.S.R.*, 43 (1955), pp. 535–45.

figures of the cross in the material world, such as a ship's rigging, a carpenter's adze, the human form and face, the military standard. "Nothing in the world can exist and form a whole (κοινωνίαν ἔχειν) without this sign." In the list he includes the plough: "Can the earth be ploughed (ἀροῦται) without it [the cross]?" The comparison is explained by the fact that the old pattern of plough was indeed cross-shaped, the beam corresponding to the upright, the share and tail forming either end of the horizontal piece.[8]

It is known that Irenaeus often took his cue from Justin, and that this is one of the places where he did so is made probable by the following fact. We have seen that he started from Isaias 2. 3–4. In a first part that we have hitherto passed over, he refers the beating of swords into ploughshares to the peaceful attitude of Christians (IV, 34, 4). Now this interpretation is found in Justin: "We have turned the weapons of war into ploughs and husbandmen's tools, for the cultivation of godliness, justice, kindliness, faith and hope" (*Dial.*, cx, 3).

More yet. Twice there occurs in the passage of Irenaeus an expression which we have not yet considered. We read of the Word of God "turning the swords and spears of warfare into tools of peace, into ploughs that he himself has made, into sickles that he has provided for the harvest" (IV, 34, 4). And a little further on, "It is he who has made the plough". Justin again furnishes the explanation: "When Jesus came to the Jordan he was believed to be the son of Joseph the carpenter; he himself passed as a carpenter, for while he was among men he made (εἰργάζετο) the things that carpenters make, ploughs (ἄροτρα) and yokes (ζυγά), teaching the symbols of justice

[8] See Daremberg-Saglio, *D.A.G.R.*, p. 353.

and active life" (*Dial.*, LXXXVIII, 8). This passage evidently
bears a relation to the commentary on Isaias 2. 3–4 quoted
above. It has even been proposed to correct the common-
place "things that carpenters make" (τεκτονικὰ ὄργανα)
to "weapons of war" (πολεμικὰ ὄργανα), which would
make the reference more explicit.

But the important thing is the appearance of a new
theme: Jesus the carpenter as a maker of ploughs. This is
found also in the *Gospel of Thomas* (XIII, 1), and it is quite
possible that it was the application of Isaias' prophecy to
Christ that gave it birth. It would not be a solitary case.
Several details of gospel folklore come from Isaias in this
way: the ox and the ass at the crib (Is. 1. 3), the cave of the
nativity (33. 16; LXX version),[9] the kings and their camels
(60. 6). It may be that our theme originated in the passage
of Justin; in any case it is quite certain that Irenaeus got it
from him.

It should be noticed, too, that Justin and Irenaeus apply
the prophecy to Jesus in a twofold way. On the one hand,
it is taken in the Matthaean sense, that is, applied to a
mere detail in the story of Jesus's life, as Matthew does with
Micheas 5. 2: "And thou Bethlehem, the land of Juda . . .",
or Osee 11. 1: "Out of Egypt have I called my son."
On the other hand, the narrative detail itself signifies a
spiritual reality, that of Jesus teaching holiness and charity
to men, which answers to a messianic and spiritual interpretation. That in a sentence is the theme of Christ as
ploughwright.

In the second part of his exegesis of Isaias 2. 3–4, dealing
with the allegory of the plough, Irenaeus seems to have
been following Justin no less than in the first part. The
only difference is that, whereas Justin treats the two

[9] See Justin, *Dial.*, LXXVIII, 6.

matters in separate passages, Irenaeus deals with them together in one place; but that is in accordance with his synthesizing habit.[10] It may be added that, though Justin does not mention Isaias 2. 3–4 in his passage on the allegory of the plough, it was most probably in his mind, for in general he uses symbols which have a biblical reference. For instance, in this very passage, pointing out the figure of a cross made by the nose and eyebrows, he refers to Lam. 4. 20.

Thus Justin provides an earlier reference than Irenaeus to the cruciform symbolism of the plough. This symbolism was carried on, and there is continuous evidence of its place in tradition. The *Acts of Peter* (20) include the plough (*aratrum*) in a list of Christ's titles. Minucius Felix borrows Justin's list of cosmic symbols of the cross, and he mentions the plough: "When a man holds up the yoke (*iugum*) it is the sign of the cross" (*Octavius*, 29). Mgr Pellegrino contrasts this symbolism with that of Justin, on the ground that one refers to a yoke and the other to a plough.[11] But this seems to me to be a misunderstanding: the figure is formed by the yoke or beam, making the longer arm, combined with the tail prolonged by the share, the whole forming the plough.[12]

Among the Latins in the fourth century Gregory of Elvira includes the plough among the names of Christ: "He is called 'plough' because our stony hearts are subjected to the sign of his cross to be prepared for the seeds they need" (*De fide orth.*, 6; *P.L.*, 20, 43A). This agrees with Irenaeus, for whom the plough is not only a figure of the cross but

[10] The parallel of the plough and the cross apropos of Isaias 2. 3–4 is also found in Eutropius, *De solstic. et aequinoct.*; *P.L.* Suppl., I, 565.

[11] *M. Minucii Felicis Octavius*, p. 282.

[12] Hippolytus shows Christ carrying the cross, like a plough, on his shoulder, and tilling the Church with it (*Ben. Isaac*; *P.O.*, 27, pp. 89–91).

of the Word himself. Cassian writes later: "Let us culti-
vate our hearts with the plough, that is, with the thought of
the cross" (*Coll.*, I, 22). For the symbolism of the shape of
the cross Dölger[13] refers to a text of the Syrian Ephraem,
which we give here though we shall have to examine it
again later on: "Christ's field is tilled; no weed can grow
there; it is ploughed with the plough of the cross and
every thorn is rooted up" (*On the Resurrection of Lazarus*,
II; *B.K.V.*, XXXVII, p. 176). Clement of Alexandria calls
Christ "ploughman" (ἀροτήρ. *Paed.*, III, 12, 101, 3:
G.C.S., p. 291, l. 19).

Maximus of Turin[14] gives a more detailed description
of the plough: "When he gets ready to turn over his land
in quest of food to sustain life, the good ploughman does
not seek to do so by any other means than by the sign of
the cross. When he fixes the share (*dentale*) to his plough,
secures the mould-boards (*aures*) and attaches the handle
(*stiva*), he imitates the form of the cross (*figuram crucis*). In
fact, the structure (*compactio*) is a picture of the Lord's
passion" (*Hom.*, 50; *P.L.*, 57, 342B). This describes a
Roman plough exactly.[15] Maximus seems to see a symbol
of the cross in each part of the plough. This would be
especially true of the mould-boards, one on either side of
the share, which pushed the loosened soil aside. And in
addition the whole thing (*compactio*) would in its turn be
the figure.[16]

The search for evidence of the cross-symbolism of the

---

[13] "Profane und religiöse Brandmarkung der Tiere", in *A.C.*, III, pp. 36–8.
[14] See H. Rahner, *Griechische Mythen in christlicher Deutung*, p. 86.
(English translation by Brian Battershaw, *Greek Myths and Christian
Mystery* [London, 1963], p. 56.)
[15] Daremberg-Saglio, *D.A.G.R.*, I, 355–6.
[16] Among the Greeks, St Nilus writes: "We hold the handle of the plough,
keeping the form of the cross" (*Monast. exercit.*, 6; *P.G.*, 79, 725A.

plough on pictorial monuments had until recently been fruitless. An engraved stone in the gallery at Florence, reproduced in Daremberg-Saglio (I, 353), shows the cross-form of the Greek plough in a striking way: but the piece is not Christian. All that Dom Leclercq found to mention is a sarcophagus in the Lateran Museum. It shows Adam and Eve, Daniel among the lions, the Good Shepherd and a ploughman leading a yoke of oxen: the plough is visible and vaguely resembles a cross. But there is no reason to suppose that this was the object of the representation. Once again recent Palestinian discoveries have a bearing on the question. They show that the plough's cruciform symbolism was known to Judaic Christianity, and that Justin must have got it from that.[17]

There is still one element in Irenaeus's text to be explained, and that is the work of the plough and its symbolism. In the first part, it represents the works of peace as opposed to those of war. This is Justin's idea. Later on it signifies "the first seed-time of man, who was patterned on Adam" (IV, 34, 4). But here there is no question of the plough as the cross; this appears only in the final passage: "The Lord . . . has finally shown forth the plough, wood combined with iron, and so has weeded (*expurgauit*) his land: for the 'materialized' Word, made one with flesh and fixed in the way it has been, has cleared (*emundauit*) the untilled (*siluestrem*) earth."

The idea and its symbolism are quite clear. The plough gets rid of weeds: that is what it is for, it opens out the ground and cuts the noxious growths at their root. At the second sowing, the Word-made-flesh has to root out the weeds of sin before broadcasting the new seed. That is just what the cross is for, to destroy sin, as we found in

[17] See B. Bagatti, in *Osservatore Romano*, 6 August 1960, p. 4.

Ephraem a few pages back. This symbolism brings us to a new group of texts which go to confirm the symbolism of the plough as cross. In the *Paschal Homily* inspired by Hippolytus (and published by P. Nautin), we read (57): "Christ was crowned with thorns, blotting out the earth's ancient curse and by his divine head rooting up (ἐξημερῶν) the abundant thorns that are the outcome of sin."

Nautin's comment on this passage is: "Thorns grew on earth as a result of sin (Gen. 3. 17–18). Christ suffered the thorns in order to deliver us from this olden curse: on the cross he is the plough which rids the earth of the thorns of sin, of which those of the field are a symbol" (*S.C.*, pp. 98–9). This goes beyond the letter of the text, but it is the most convincing explanation. The image of the plough is not explicitly stated, but it is not far off, for it is the only one that fits exactly: the proper meaning of ἐξημερόω is in fact "to clear land". So here we find the image of the cross as plough in the praise of the cross which is part of the Easter preaching, side by side with other pieces of symbolism which are met in Hippolytus' text.[18]

So the signifying of the cross by the plough in Irenaeus seems well established. Perhaps it can help towards solving a famous puzzle of ancient epigraphy, the magic square. Many interpretations of this have been attempted, particularly by Father de Jerphanion and, more recently, by Jérôme Carcopino, who sums up previous work on it.[19]

[18] See also Jerome, *Com. Is.*, II, 4; *P.L.*, 24, 46BC. There is a mysterious passage in the *Odes of Solomon* (XXIII, 10–13; Bernard, p. 97) which might be connected with our theme. It speaks of a wheel which mows down, fells, uproots forests, and drives a road: there are some who see a symbol of the cross in this.

[19] *Études d'histoire chrétienne* (Paris, 1953), pp. 11–91. See also J. Vendryès, "Une Hypothèse sur le carré magique", in *C.R.A.I.B.L.* (1953), pp. 198–206.

Two things seem to have been established by the solutions offered. The first is that the figure makes a cross both by its general arrangement and by the place of the Ts, themselves figures of the cross.[20] In this way:

```
        S A T O R
        A R E P O
        T E N E T
        O P E R A
        R O T A S
```

The second point is that the strange word *arepo* appears to be connected with the Celtic word *arepennis*, which means "acre" (French *arpent*) and has the sense of "a plough".[21]

It is curious that Professor Carcopino should emphasize these two things without connecting them with one another. Perhaps the symbol of the cross as plough did not strike him as being used in the district wherein he finds the origin of the square. But that district is the Rhône valley, in the time of St Irenaeus; and our study certainly proves that Irenaeus knew this symbol. Surely this is a confirmation of Professor Carcopino's hypothesis, associating the square with the country of Irenaeus, and of our hypothesis, which detects the cross in Irenaeus's passage about the plough.

[20] See H. Rahner, "Das Mystische Tau", in *Z.K.T.*, 75 (1953), pp. 385-410.

[21] Ernout-Meillet, *Dict. étym. langue lat.* (Paris, 1939), p. 70.

There is something further in the passage of Irenaeus which seems to have an equivalent in the magic square. Irenaeus says: "He who joined the beginning with the end, and is the Lord of both, has shown forth the plough at the end" (IV, 34, 4). Professor Carcopino has made the interesting suggestion that the letters A and O, on either side of the T at the end of each of the branches of the cross in the square, are the Alpha and Omega which in St John's Apocalypse symbolize Christ as beginning and end (*op. cit.*, pp. 40–1). In the passage from Irenaeus, this symbolism has an anti-gnostic sense. The Gnostics interpreted John 4. 37, "One sows, another reaps...", as opposing the Demiurge who creates to the Christ who redeems; and Irenaeus declares on the contrary that they are one. As the cross, symbolized by the plough, has been shown forth in the beginning, at the first seed-time, so it is in the end, at the final weeding.

Accordingly, Irenaeus's text gives a clue not only for the connection between cross and plough but also for that of this symbol with Alpha and Omega. It also shows the association of the whole thing with an anti-gnostic environment. In particular it may be noticed that the image of the seed and the sower (*sator*) connects with the importance of this theme in Valentinian Gnosticism—it is not found elsewhere in early times. This attempted explanation presupposes that the connection of the square with Irenaeus's sphere is well founded—a view that is disputed by some competent critics. And in addition, so many explanations of the square have been offered that it behoves one to be diffident. But if Professor Carcopino's hypothesis be right, Irenaeus's use of the plough as a symbol of the cross is a notable confirmation of it.

7

The Star of Jacob

The importance of collections of *testimonia* in the earliest
Christian community was pointed out long ago, particularly by Rendel Harris, and Mgr Cerfaux has shown how
often early theology was expressed in terms of some of
these texts. The Qumran discoveries provide confirmation
of this, for they prove that similar collections existed in
Judaism. More remarkable still, they were partly made up
of the same texts. This makes the *testimonia* of considerable
value in tracing the connection of Christianity with its
original environment, as we will try to show by reference
to the Book of Numbers, 24. 17.

The presence in the primitive *testimonia* of Balaam's
prophecy about "the star of Jacob" has been remarked
for a long time. The text is mentioned by Justin and
Irenaeus who, it is agreed, made use of older collections.
At the same time the text is not explicitly quoted in the
New Testament, though some scholars have claimed to
detect allusions to it. This, however, is disputed; but it
seems that the matter may be considered as decided, from
the fact that the text is, perhaps, the most frequently
quoted in the Qumran writings. It therefore had a
special popularity at the time when the New Testament
was being formed. We must first establish this point.

In those Qumran manuscripts which have been published, Numbers 24. 17 occurs a number of times. In
D.S.W. it is quoted in full and applied to David (xi, 6);

and it is possible that *D.S.W.* is referring to it in VI, 6 and
XVI, I.[1] The *Benediction of the Leader of the Congregation*
uses a collection of *testimonia* about the sceptre (*shebet*) in
which Isaias II. I and Numbers 24. 17 are associated
(*I Q. Ben.*, V, 27).[2] Yet more notable is the occurrence of
Numbers 24. 15–17 in a group of *testimonia* where it is
associated with Deuteronomy 5. 28–9 and 33. 8–11.[3]
Notice in the last two cases that the text is grouped with
certain others.

Finally, there is a particularly interesting mention in the
Damascus Document. Here is the passage in full: "When
the two houses of Israel separated, Ephraim left Juda.
Those who turned aside were put to the sword, but those
who remained steadfast escaped to the northern country,
according to the word, 'I will banish the *sikkuth* (tent)
of your king and the *kiyyun* (pedestal) of your idols
beyond the tents of Damascus' [Amos 5. 26–7]. As the
books of the Law, so is the tent of the king, as it is said:
'I will raise up the tabernacle of David, that is fallen'
[Amos 9. 11]. The king is the assemblage and the *kiyyun*
of the idols are the books of the prophets, whose words
Israel set at naught. The star is he who searches the Law,
who came to the region of Damascus, as it is written,
'A star shall rise out of Jacob and a sceptre shall spring up
from Israel' [Num. 24. 17]. The sceptre is the leader of
the whole gathering: when he arises, he will destroy all the
children of Seth" (VII, 12–21).

We shall have to come back to this text, and only three
things need be said here. In the first place, the transition

[1] J. Carmignac, "Les citations de l'A.T. dans 'La Guerre des Fils de
Lumière contre les Fils de Ténèbres'" in *R.B.*, 63 (1956), p. 385.

[2] *Qumran Cave*, I, pp. 128–9.

[3] Allegro, "Further Messianic References in Qumran Literature",
in *J.B.L.*, 65 (1956), pp. 182–7.

from the Amos 5 quotation to that from Numbers is explained by the fact that the authentic text of Amos reads "*Kiyyun*, your idol, the star of your gods". The *C.D.C.* quotes loosely, but alludes to the authentic text. Secondly, "the star", which refers to David in *D.S.W.* and to the Davidic Messiah in *I Q. Test.*, is here oddly applied to "him who searches the Law"[4] in the land of Damascus, whether it be the Master of Justice who is in question or someone else. Lastly, we note that the two quotations from Amos are found in the Acts of the Apostles. The second (Acts 15. 16–17), which incidentally is found in a collection of Qumran *testimonia* (IV Q. *Flor.*, 3),[5] comes from the mouth of James, with reference to the conversion of the Gentiles. The text given in Acts differs from the Septuagint, but is the same as that in *C.D.C.* and in IV Q. *Flor.*

The other quotation is Amos 5. 26–7, occurring in Stephen's discourse (Acts 7. 42–3). It is difficult to imagine that Stephen could have used so peculiar a passage without dependence on *C.D.C.* or the Qumran writings. He quotes it according to the Septuagint, but with one strange alteration: instead of "beyond Damascus", the text says "beyond Babylon". Now it is very curious that, after studying the Amos quotation in *C.D.C.*, C. Rabinowitz thinks that Damascus there really denotes Babylon.[6] One is tempted to believe that this interpretation of Amos was already existent in Jewish exegesis at the time of Christ. We may notice finally that this Amos text is found in Justin (*Dial.*, XXII, 3–4).

But let us continue our inquiry, and examine the

[4] See H. Riesenfeld, *Jésus transfiguré*, p. 227.
[5] Allegro, *loc. cit.*, p. 176.
[6] "The Damascus (Zadokite) Fragments", in *J.B.L.*, 73 (1954), pp. 26, 33.

Christian *testimonia*.[7] A study of them is decisive. The prophecy in Numbers 24. 17 occurs several times. The *Testaments of the Twelve Patriarchs* is a document of special interest, because it is a link between Qumran and Judaic Christianity. Whether, with M. de Jonge, we look on it as a properly Christian work or whether we are faithful to the theory of interpolations, it remains that it is a Christian document in the form in which we have it. And in it the Numbers prophecy is twice quoted, and in important contexts.

The first time is in the *Testament of Levi*, 18, 3. It is given thus: "Ἀνατελεῖ ἄστρον αὐτοῦ (= ἱερέα καινόν) ἐν οὐρανῷ ὡς βασιλέως φωτίζων φῶς γνώσεως". De Jonge observes that the way in which the quotation is presented seems to suggest an allusion to Matthew 2. 2, the star of the Wise Men.[8] Perhaps so; in the Numbers text, the star denotes the Messiah himself; here, it is a star that appears and is a sign of the coming of the Messiah. This is emphasized by the words ἐν οὐρανῷ, which are found again with reference to the star of Bethlehem in Ignatius (*Eph.*, xix, 2) and Justin (*Dial.*, cvi, 4). The allusion to "the king" also recalls Matthew 2. 2 as ἄστρον αὐτοῦ does αὐτοῦ τὸν ἀστέρα in the same passage. The end of the quotation is borrowed from the Septuagint version of Osee 10. 12. The application of the star prophecy to the Messiah-priest is not found in Qumran documents, except perhaps in *C.D.C.* It seems to imply the Christian unity of the Messiah, who is both priest and king.

Numbers 24. 17 occurs a second time in the *Testament*

[7] Outside Qumran, Num. 24. 17 is quoted by Philo in his only messianic passage (*Praem.*, 16, 95). See A. Chevallier, *L'Esprit et le Messie dans le bas judaïsme et le N.T.* (Paris, 1958), p. 39.

[8] *The Testaments of the XII Patriarchs*, p. 154.

of Juda, XXIV, 1: "'Aνατελεῖ ἄστρον ἐξ Ἰακὼβ καὶ ἀναστήσεται ἄνθρωπος ὡς ἥλιος δικαιοσύνης". The text agrees with the Septuagint, which reads ἄνθρωπος for *shebet*. Notice the approximation to Malachias 4. 2, a text that is found in the collection of Christian *testimonia*; the approximation may be implied again at the end of the *Testament of Levi*, XVIII, 3, "ἐν ἡλίῳ ἡμέρα".

That Numbers 24. 17 was included in ancient collections of *testimonia* is further attested by the use made of it by the early authors who used these *testimonia*. The first is Justin, who mentions "star" amongst Christ's traditional titles on the strength of this text: "He is called star (ἄστρον) by Moses himself, Orient (ἀνατολή) by Zacharias, rod (ῥάβδος), flower (ἄνθος), corner-stone (λίθος ἀκρογωνιαῖος)" (*Dial.*, CXXVI, 1). 'Ράβδος and ἄνθος come from Isaias 11. 1, which we have already found connected with Numbers 24. 17 in Qumran writings.[9]

This convergence appears in another passage of Justin: "Another prophet, Isaias, announces the same thing in other terms: 'A star will rise out of Jacob and a flower will grow on the stem (ῥίζα) of Jesse....' This shining star that rose, this flower that grew on Jesse's stem, is Christ" (*I Apol.*, XXXII, 12–13). Here Numbers 24. 17 and Isaias 11. 1 are combined in one quotation and attributed to Isaias. This kind of composite quotation is common in the earliest Christian writings, especially in Pseudo-Barnabas, and is characteristic of texts drawn from *testimonia*.

A third quotation from Justin introduces other elements: "Moses himself gave us to understand that he must needs arise like a star from Abraham's race. These are the words: 'A star shall rise out of Jacob and a leader (ἡγούμενος) from Israel.' And another Scripture says:

[9] On this connection, cf. Chevallier, *op. cit.*, pp. 32–4.

'Behold, a man: Orient is his name' [Zach. 6. 12]. And so
when a star rose in the sky at his birth, as it is written in the
memorials of his apostles, the wise men of Arabia recognized the event, 'and they came and worshipped him'"
(*Dial.*, CVI, 4). The translation ἡγούμενος for *shebet* will be
noticed. Justin here parts company with the Septuagint
and comes closer to the Hebrew text. Perhaps he was
influenced by Genesis 49. 10, which forms part of the
same group,[10] where in the Septuagint ἡγούμενος is the
rendering of "ruler's staff". The word also figures in
Micheas 5.2 [1], as quoted in Matthew 2. 6.

Here the prophecy in Numbers suggests two interesting
comparisons. The first is with Zacharias 6. 12, where the
Septuagint has ἀνατολή for *semah*, that is, "shoot". It is
the same in 3. 8 and in Jeremias 23. 5. But Justin under-
stands the word to mean "east", which is equally possible.
As H. Schlier has said, it seems that this may be due to the
influence of ἀνατελεῖ in Numbers 24. 17, with which the
testimonia grouped it.[11] The sense Justin gives to Zacharias
6. 12 would then be one more allusion to Numbers 24. 17.

But this allusion seems to be older than Justin. On the
one hand, Philo gives ἀνατολή as one of the names of the
Logos, understanding it in the sense of "east". This
seems certainly to be referred to Zacharias 6. 12 interpreted in relation to Numbers 24. 17. And no doubt the
phrase ἀνατολὴ ἐξ ὕψους in Luke 1. 78 must be explained in
the same way. The expression indeed seems to refer to the
designation of the Messiah as the "shoot which comes
from God" according to Zacharias and Jeremias. And on
the other hand, Luke 1. 79 shows that the word is associated
with the idea of light. So Luke 1. 78 also would include

[10] See *I Apol.*, XXXII, I.
[11] Ἀνατολή, *T.W.N.T.*, I, p. 355.

an indirect allusion to Numbers 24. 17 and have to be added to our dossier of references to that text.[12]

But there is another element of great interest in Justin's text: the bringing together of Matthew 2. 1 and Numbers 24. 17. We have seen that the *Testament of Levi* related the "star of Jacob" with the "star of the Wise Men". Justin now goes further and sees in the magian star the fulfilment of Balaam's prophecy. We must look at the relationship of these two themes.

The various elements we have so far brought together show that Numbers 24. 17 occurred with marked continuity in a number of texts immediately preceding and following the New Testament. It is therefore certain that the text was included in the *testimonia* that primitive Christianity took over from the Qumran community. The presence of the star on Judaeo-Christian monuments confirms this. So it is *a priori* certain that the text formed part of the dossier used by the writers of the New Testament, though it is never quoted explicitly therein. But are there not allusions to it? We will examine certain possibilities.

The first is in St John's Apocalypse, where the theme of the morning star (ὁ ἀστὴρ ὁ πρωϊνός) occurs twice. This expression proves nothing by itself. But in the first passage (2. 26–8) the mention of the morning star is preceded by a quotation from Psalm 2. 8–9: "I will give him power over the nations, and he shall rule them with a rod (ῥάβδος) of iron." Now the star and the sceptre are associated in Numbers 24. 17, and that text formed part of a dossier on the sceptre which we have met at Qumran, including Genesis 49. 10 and Isaias 11. 1–5 (*I Q. Ben.*,

[12] See P. Benoît, "L'enfance de Jean-Baptiste selon Luc 1", in *N.T.S.*, 3 (1956), pp. 186–7.

v, 24–8). It must have comprised Psalm 2. 8–9. Consequently it seems that the morning star also must be interpreted in relation to these *testimonia* and be referred to Numbers 24. 17.

This is fully confirmed by the second passage in the Apocalypse, 22. 16: "I am the root (ῥίζα) and stock of David, the bright and morning star (ὁ ἀστὴρ ὁ λαμπρὸς ὁ πρωϊνός)." The phrase "stock of David" confirms that "the root" is here a quotation from Isaias 11. 1; and this text is associated with Numbers 24. 17 in the *testimonia*, as witness Justin's passage given above wherein the two quotations are combined in one and attributed to Isaias. Surely this composite quotation is the basis of Apocalypse 22. 16. The morning star here must then refer to Numbers 24. 17, confirming that it is the same in Apocalypse 2. 28.

One may ask whether the epithet πρωϊνός is not a further confirmatory allusion to Numbers 24. 17. In this text we read "ἀνατελεῖ ἄστρον"; and, as has been pointed out above, the verb ἀνατέλλω suggests the idea of ἀνατολή. Now ἀνατολή can indicate a place, and it then means "east" or "orient". But it can also indicate time, and then signifies "sunrise" or "dawn". In this sense the word comes close to πρωΐ; and, as ἀνατολή has no usual corresponding adjective, it is understandable that πρωϊνός should be used as a substitute.

This probably allows us to see a reference to Numbers 24. 17 in another New-Testament text, 2 Peter 1. 19. After recalling what happened at the Transfiguration, the writer goes on: "It is with good reason that you are paying so much attention to that [prophetical] word; it will go on shining, like a lamp in some darkened room, until the dawn breaks and the day-star rises (φωσφόρος ἀνατείλῃ) in your hearts." The line of thought seems to be this: the Transfiguration anticipates eschatological light; we look forward to the coming of that light, relying on the prophetical word which tells us that the day will dawn and the morning star appear. In other words, it looks as if day and day-star must be referred to προφητικὸς λόγος.

The two expressions are associated in the ancient dossiers, as Justin testifies. We may compare his *Dialogue*, c, 4: "He is called Wisdom, Day, Dawn", with CXXVI, 1: "Wisdom he is called by Solomon, Star by Moses, Dawn by Zacharias." Clearly we have the same sequence, and star and day are the key words of the dossier. Their association in 2 Peter 1. 19 appears to presuppose this dossier. I have considered elsewhere the biblical texts relevant to the title Day.[13] That of Star comes from Numbers 24. 17, as Justin says explicitly, and so it comes from the same place in 2 Peter 1. 19. Furthermore, φωσφόρος ἀνατείλῃ seems to be an echo of ἄστρον ἀνατελεῖ. This is not without interest for the interpretation of the Transfiguration itself, which the writer of the epistle sees as the anticipated fulfilment of the prophecy in Numbers 24. 17, that is, of the glory of the Davidic Messiah.

Moreover, the analogy of the contexts in which the star is mentioned in these various passages and those in which we find it mentioned by Qumran and the Judaeo-Christian *testimonia* seems to leave no room for doubt that in either case the star is connected with Numbers 24. 17. There remains one last text that presents a special problem, Matthew 2. 2, 9–10, the appearing of the star to the Wise Men. Eric Burrows thinks the account can imply a reminiscence of Numbers 24. 17.[14] He also observes that Balaam comes ἀπὸ ἀνατολῶν (Num. 23. 7) and the same

[13] *Théologie du judéo-christianisme*, pp. 222–8.
[14] *The Oracles of Jacob and Balaam* (London, 1938), p. 98.

phrase is used of the Magi in Matthew 2. 1. This indicates a connection between Balaam and the Magi to which we shall return. Furthermore, Krister Stendahl notes that Numbers 24. 17 is the only place in the Old Testament where "rise" is expressed by ἀνατέλλω; consequently the ἐν τῇ ἀνατολῇ of Matthew 2. 2, 9 can be referred to it.[15] It follows that ἐντῇ ἀνατολῇ must signify "at its rising", and not "in the east", which would be ἐν ταῖς ἀνατολαῖς. And so we may believe, with J. Legrand, that the Wise Men, who came from the east, saw the star shining in the west above Bethlehem.[16]

This hypothesis appears to be confirmed by the fact that the star of the Magi was brought into relation with Balaam's prophecy in the earliest tradition. We have seen evidence of this in the *Testament of Levi* and in Justin. It is found again in Irenaeus (*Adv. haer.*, III, 9, 2 and *Dem.*, 58; *P.O.*, 12, p. 704). But Origen above all provides something of great interest, when he brings the Wise Men into relation with Balaam: "The Magi, seeing God's sign in the heavens, looked for its meaning. I think they knew the prophecies of Balaam that are recorded by Moses" (*Contra Cels.*, I, 60).

And elsewhere: "If Balaam's prophecies were included in the sacred books by Moses, there was yet stronger reason for their being accepted by the inhabitants of Mesopotamia: for Balaam had a great reputation amongst those people, who are known as his disciples in magic. It is to him that tradition attributes the origin of magi in eastern lands, and the magi had in their country the text of all Balaam's prophecies, including, 'A star shall rise

[15] *The School of St Matthew* (Uppsala, 1954), p. 136.
[16] "Vidimus stellam eius in oriente", in *Clergy Monthly*, 23 (1959), pp. 377–84.

out of Jacob and a man shall spring up from Israel'. The Magi were familiar with this text. So, when Jesus was born, they recognized the star and understood that the prophecy was fulfilled" (*Hom. Num.*, XIII, 7).

The interesting point here is not the fantastic legend that the magi had preserved Balaam's oracles, but rather the connection between the magi and the prophet. Here Origen is testifying to Eastern traditions which were anterior to him, as Franz Cumont and Joseph Bidez have shown: in certain Eastern traditions Balaam was identified with Zoroaster, founder of the magi.[17] The consequence was that Balaam himself was regarded as a magus.[18] At once we see a new relationship between the prophecy in Numbers 24. 17 and Matthew 2. 2. It is no longer the star alone which is common to both, but also the fact that each is concerned with magi, that is to say, Iranian priests.

We have gathered together the allusions to Numbers 24. 17 provided by ancient Christian writings. We must now consider whether it be possible to give precision to their context, to ascertain the *Sitz im Leben* of the use of the prophecy in primitive Christianity. We may begin with the last pointer we reached. Bringing together the above text and Matthew 2. 2, Origen emphasized the relationship of the Messiah and the star to a *milieu* that was in contact with the magi. This is confirmed by other texts.

The first of them is from Ignatius of Antioch in his letter to the Christians at Ephesus, XIX, 2–3: "How, then, were these mysteries [Mary's virginity, Christ's birth and passion] revealed to the ages? A star shone in the sky, brighter than all other stars; its light was indescribable

---

[17] *Les Mages hellénisés*, I, pp. 48–9.
[18] H. J. Schoeps, *Aus frühchristlicher Zeit* (Tübingen, 1960), pp. 249–54.

22, 2), occupied by preaching and teaching. The symbolic elements are the same, but the explanations differ.

In addition, we find among the Gnostics yet more conclusive parallels with Ebionites and Catholics in the matter that concerns us. Giving an account of the teaching of Theodotus, Clement of Alexandria writes: "For him, the apostles have been substituted for the twelve signs of the zodiac; for, since these govern generation, the apostles are the directors of regeneration" (*Exc. Theod.*, 25, 2). In his edition of Clement's work (*Sources chrétiennes*, 1948), Father F. M. M. Sagnard rightly refers in a note to the *Clementine Homilies*, II, 23. The context there is indeed just the same. The substitution of the apostles for the *Kosmokratores* and of evangelical freedom for enslavement to destiny is admirably expressed, whatever the author's substratum. And the twelve zodiacal signs are explicitly mentioned.[7]

These speculations reappear in later gnostic treatises. *Pistis Sophia* is full of them. The twelve aeons make up the day; noon is Adamas, the twelfth aeon (67; G.C.S., p. 93, ll. 34 ff.): this is an allusion to Psalm 90. 6. A notable point is the opposition between the twelve regions of the aeons and the thirteenth, which was higher than they (50; G.C.S., p. 58). We have not met this type of opposition before. It can be found in an orthodox perspective in St Ephraem: the apostles are twelve days, Christ is the thirteenth (*Hymn. Epiph.*, I, 11). Opposition of this sort appears as purely eastern, which shows that the symbolism we are examining is not specifically Graeco-Roman.

There is another passage in *Pistis Sophia* deserving attention. It is a comment on Mat. 19. 28: "You shall sit on twelve thrones, judging the twelve tribes of Israel."

[7] See also *Adv. haer.*, I, 17, 1, where they represent the aeons.

In this passage the writer sees the restoration of the twelve deliverers to the celestial regions of each one, and the twelve apostles' part in that restoration (ἀποκατάστασις) (50; G.C.S., p. 57, ll. 7 ff.). There is a very similar exegesis in Origen (*Com. Mat.*, xv, 24), inspired by Genesis 49. 28 and Mat. 19. 28. The twelve tribes typify the celestial peoples, the fathers of the twelve tribes are twelve stars: the celestial peoples will be judged by the twelve apostles. The two exegeses are exactly parallel. Origen is even more explicit than *Pistis Sophia* in assimilating the twelve patriarchs to twelve stars which preside over the twelve celestial regions; this is clearly an allusion to the zodiac.

Another late gnostic work, published by Carl Schmidt, also gives an interesting pointer. The Only-Begotten is shown therein holding in his right hand the twelve fatherhoods, figuring the twelve apostles, and in his left the thirty powers (δυνάμεις). All these powers encircle the Only-Begotten like a crown, according to David's word: "Thou shalt bless the crown of the year of thy goodness" (Ps. 64. 12). And in fact the twelve apostles multiplied by the thirty powers corresponds to the twelve months of thirty days that make a year. Here again it is clear that underlying the author's speculation there is a parallelism of the twelve apostles and twelve months, corresponding to a symbolism of the Only-Begotten as the perfect year. The quoting of Psalm 64. 12 here is of special interest, for this text was certainly included in the dossier of the Word as the perfect year.

There is confirmation of this in a group of texts connected with the epithet ἐνιαύσιος, "one year old", which is applied in Exodus 12. 5 to the paschal lamb. Gregory Nazianzen comments on the epithet thus: "He is called 'of one year' as sun of justice, either as come from on high, or as limited in his visible being and returning to himself, as blessed crown of goodness [Ps. 64. 12] and in everything equal and like to himself" (*Or.*, 45, 13; *P.G.*, 36, 641A–B). But some Latin writers relate the epithet to Christ's one year of ministry. Thus Gregory of Elvira: "He is called *anniculus* because after his baptism by John in the Jordan, the time of his preaching being accomplished, Christ suffered, in accordance with David's prophecy: 'Thou shalt bless the crown of the year of thy goodness'" (*Tract.*, 9; *P.L. Suppl.*, 1, 413).

The theme is treated at greater length by Gaudentius of Brescia: "He is *anniculus* because one year elapsed from his baptism for us in the Jordan to the day of his passion. . . . That was the 'acceptable year of the Lord' [Is. 61. 2], of which Jesus, reading in the synagogue, declared that it had been written of himself in the book of Isaias [Luke 4. 21]. That was what the rejoicing prophet extolled in the psalm: 'Thou shalt bless the crown of the year of thy goodness'. It was the triumphant circle blessed by Christ's deeds of goodness" (*Serm.*, 3; *P.L.*, 20, 865B–6B). Here we have a western tradition concerning one year as the duration of Christ's public life which is found in Tertullian and persisted until St Augustine; it parallels what is found in Clement at Alexandria and in the Gnostics. But the interest of the above passage is that it is the first we have in which Psalm 64. 12 and Isaias 61. 2 occur together: they are the two chief texts for the theme of Christ as year.

To reach a conclusion, let us go back to the starting-point of this brief inquiry. In the Pseudo-Clementine writings, in the gnostic Theodotus, in Hippolytus of Rome, the twelve apostles are symbolized by the twelve

hours, the twelve months, the twelve signs of the zodiac.
There is no ground for supposing that these different
writers depended on one another. But all of them appear
to direct us towards a Judaeo-Christian *milieu*. Can the
origin of this symbolism be explained by referring back
to such a *milieu*? If so, we should be justified in thinking
that we have here a very early symbolism, which later
survived among a limited number of Christian thinkers.

It looks as if this was the case. The symbolism we are
considering indeed seems to rest on Jewish ideas current in
the environment in which Christianity began. We see in
the first place that the signs of the zodiac were familiar
forms of representation in Hellenistic Judaism. But the
same would appear to be true of Palestinian Judaism too.
Erwin Goodenough has proved that the zodiacal figures
were represented in synagogues of Palestine from the
first century before the Christian era.[8] Later on, in the
synagogue at Beth Alpha, they are accompanied by their
Hebrew names. We know from Epiphanius that "the
Pharisees had translated the names of the twelve signs into
Hebrew".[9] And, when describing the veil of the Temple,
Josephus explains that the whole sky was represented on it,
except the signs of the zodiac, which shows that their
representation might have been usual.[10]

It was therefore very tempting to connect this symbol-
ogy of the twelve zodiacal signs with that of the twelve
Jewish patriarchs. And in fact in Philo—at the very time
of Christ—we see the number twelve used sometimes with
a cosmic reference to the signs of the zodiac, sometimes

[8] *Jewish Symbols*, I, pp. 203, 217, 219, 248–51, 255; VIII, pp. 167–71.
[9] *Panarion*, XVI, 2, 2; *G.C.S.*, pp. 211–12.
[10] See A. Pelletier, "La tradition synoptique du 'Voile déchiré'", in
R.S.R., 46 (1958), pp. 170 ff.

with an historical reference to the twelve patriarchs.[11] The two symbolisms were bound to converge, and that is what we find. For Philo, the two emeralds, one on each shoulder of the high priest and each bearing the names of six patriarchs, are a symbol of the signs of the zodiac (*Quaest. Ex.*, II, 109). And not only that: in explaining the meaning of the twelve stones on the metal plaque which the high priest wore on his breast, Philo makes a parallel between the patriarchs and the zodiacal signs. The following is the passage:

"The twelve gems are figures of the twelve animals of the zodiac.[12] This is the symbol of the twelve patriarchs, for their names are engraved on the stones, with the object of making them stars and as it were giving each its own constellation (ζῴδιον). More than that, each patriarch himself becomes a constellation, a sort of heavenly image, so that the patriarchs and leaders of peoples no longer walk the earth as mortals but are become celestial growths, moving in the heavens where they are planted" (*ibid.*, II, 114). Philo goes on to present them as permanent ideas, whose seal is able to stamp innumerable copies with their image.

This extraordinary passage puts forward a doctrine of the stellar immortality of the patriarchs which is specifically Philo's;[13] it recalls what Tatian rebuked the heathen for doing when they translated the animals which they worshipped into the heavens (*Disc.*, 9). But at the same time Philo bears witness here to a symbolism that is not peculiar to him. The analogy between the patriarchs and

[11] *Vita Mos.*, II, 123–4; *Her.*, 176–7.

[12] It must be remembered that the zodiac can be represented either by twelve living creatures or by twelve devices (Boll, *op. cit.*, p. 69).

[13] But see Wisdom 3. 7, according to Dupont-Sommer's interpretation.

the animals of the zodiac could find support from the fact that in the well-known prophecy of Genesis 49 Juda was compared to a lion, Issachar to a donkey, Dan to a snake, Nephtali to a hind, Benjamin to a wolf.[14] And in fact the *Book of Jubilees* (xxv, 16) assimilates the twelve patriarchs to the twelve months. Hartvig Thyen has remarked on the connections of the Jewish preaching of Christ's time with synagogue art, and he mentions the zodiac. Rabbinic tradition kept this symbolism too,[15] and it does not appear in any way to have borrowed it from Philo. It seems to have borne, not only on the twelve months, but also on the twelve hours: "Twelve princes will be begotten. The tribes will be determined by the order of the world: the day has twelve hours, the year has twelve months, the zodiac has twelve signs. As it is said: 'All these things are the tribes of Israel.'"[16]

Afterwards it was quite easy to transfer the zodiacal symbolism from the twelve patriarchs to the twelve apostles. We are fortunate enough to have a text in which this process can be seen happening, a passage in Clement of Alexandria which we have not mentioned hitherto. It concerns the symbolism of the high-priestly vesture, and Clement must be dependent on Philo: "The twelve stones arranged in fours on the breast set forth the cycle of the zodiac with its four changes of season. . . .

[14] See Goodenough, *op. cit.*, VIII, pp. 196-7, with the references.

[15] H. Thyen, *Der Stil der jüdisch-hellenistischen Homilie* (Göttingen, 1955), p. 33.—R. Eisler, *Orphisch-Dionysische Mysteriengedanke in der christlichen Antike* (Leipzig, 1925), p. 39; Goodenough, *op. cit.* VIII, pp. 197-9.

[16] Tanchuma, *Wajchi*, 16, quoted by D. Feuchtwang, "Der Tierkreis in der Tradition und im Synagogenritus", in *M.G.W.J.*, 59 (1915), p. 243. See also the words that Romanus the Hymnwriter puts into the mouth of Jacob: "A day has risen for me, having twelve hours, which are my children" (cf. Eisler, *op. cit.*, p. 39). In the Syriac *Book of Shem* this symbolism is attributed to Asaph (M. Burrows, *New Light on the Dead Sea Scrolls*).

By these are signified the just of both covenants, for if we were to say the apostles are both prophets and just we should not be deceiving ourselves" (*Strom.*, v, 6, 38, 4–5; *G.C.S.*, p. 352, ll. 7 ff.). Here we see the transition from the patriarchs to the apostles in full swing.

This is the way the history of this piece of symbolism appears to us. At the start the signs of the zodiac are used as a decorative motif in Judaeo-Hellenistic art. This leads the rabbis to comment on the design symbolically, regarding it as an image of the twelve patriarchs. In Philo this symbolism rises to a certain cosmic mysticism. The Judaeo-Christians take it up and apply it to the twelve apostles; it becomes associated with the symbolism of Christ considered as day and as year. It is met among the members of the Great Church as well as among Ebionites and Gnostics. Reciprocal influences may well have made themselves felt: Asterius, for instance, appears to depend on certain ideas borrowed from the Gnostics.[17] Side by side with the symbolism of the twelve apostles, certain others made their appearance, such as Zeno of Verona's curious application of the zodiac to the newly baptized (*P.L.*, 11, 494–5).

[17] On developments of the theme in the Middle Ages and at the Renaissance, see F. Piper, *Mythologie der christlichen Kunst*, 11, pp. 276–310.

9

The Taw *Sign*

The sign of the cross made on the forehead is one of the oldest observances of the Christian Church. St Basil mentions it, along with prayer made towards the east, among the unwritten traditions going back to the apostles. We shall show directly that this is quite likely and that the sign of the cross is connected with the primitive Judaeo-Christian community. Any analogies that may then have been looked for in the Graeco-Roman world are purely secondary considerations. We shall first list ancient liturgical uses of the cross; then we shall seek their origins; and finally we shall examine their meanings.

The first appearance of the sign of the cross is in baptismal rites,[1] and it is to this, its most ancient use, that Basil refers. Originally it was associated with the baptizing itself, either just before or just after (this is found at a very early date in the Syrian Church, which kept some very archaic usages.) That explains why ancient writers often use the sign of the cross to indicate baptism itself. For example, at the end of the second century the Abercius inscription speaks of the people "who bear the glorious seal": the word "seal" (σφραγίς) means the sign of the cross traced on the forehead.

Later, when baptismal rites were more developed, the *sphragis* was the first observance in respect of catechumens,

[1] I have gone into this subject in *The Bible and the Liturgy*, pp. 54–69. I now give some different examples.

the token of a first consecration to Christ. An African
bishop of the fourth century, Quodvultdeus, writes:
"You are not yet born anew in baptism, but you have
been conceived in the Church's womb by the sign of the
cross" (*On the Creed*, I, I). In his *Confessions*, St Augustine
relates that after his birth his mother made the sign of the
cross on his forehead and gave him a pinch of salt. But he
was not baptized until over thirty years later.

However, the use of the sign of the cross was not con-
fined to baptism: it had its place in other sacraments,
confirmation, the last anointing and the Eucharist in
particular. And, in addition, Christians signed the forehead before the chief activities of life. St John Chrysostom
says: "Everything is done by the cross. Baptism is given
by the cross—we must receive the *sphragis*—the laying on
of hands is done by the cross. Wherever we are, travelling
or at home, the cross is a great good, a saving protection,
an impregnable shield against the devil" (*Hom. Phil.*, 13,
1; *P.G.*, 62, 277).

Here we come upon the important idea that the cross
defends the baptized person against evil spirits: it makes
him inviolable and puts them to flight. The Fathers tell
numerous stories to illustrate this.[2] In particular, those
wicked spirits which are at work in heathen cults are
reduced to powerlessness by the sign of the cross. Pruden-
tius relates what happened one day when Julian the
Apostate was offering a sacrifice to Hecate. The priest who
was examining the entrails of the victim suddenly turned
pale and fell to the ground: "The prince was as terrified
as if he saw Christ in person threatening him with a
thunderbolt; blanching, he removed his diadem, and
cast an eye over the bystanders to see whether there was

[2] See *The Bible and the Liturgy*, pp. 61–3.

II

not a baptized child present who had signed his forehead with the cross, and thus upset the incantations of Zoroaster" (*Apotheosis*, 489–93). In the same way Lactantius explains that oracles and soothsayers were hindered by the presence of a Christian signed with the *sphragis* (*Div. Inst.*, v, 27). When Gregory the Wonderworker went into a pagan temple he "cleansed the pestilential atmosphere with the sign of the cross".[3]

The cross thus becomes equivalent to an exorcism. Traced on the forehead of a catechumen, it drives away the devil under whose dominion he had been. In the same way after death, when the Christian soul leaves the body and goes through the demon-infested atmosphere, the *sphragis* on his brow scatters the wicked spirits, whilst the soul that is not so marked is at their mercy: "As sheep without a shepherd are the ready prey of wild beasts, so the soul that has not the *sphragis* is at the mercy of the devil's snares."[4] "An unsealed treasure is at the mercy of thieves, a sheep without its mark is at the mercy of decoys."[5]

Not only did Christians make the cross on their foreheads with the thumb: there is evidence for the practice of actual tattooing. The custom of tattooing was known in the cults of Dionysus and Mithras, but it seems to have existed among Christians too, in respect of the sign of the cross. It is implied by St Augustine in Africa: he says that when pagans come out of the amphitheatre they recognize Christians by their clothes, their headdress and their foreheads.[6] In his *Life of Porphyry of Gaza*, Mark the Deacon (fifth century) writes of three children who fell

---

[3] Gregory of Nyssa, *Life of Gregory the Wonderworker*; P.G., 46, 916A.

[4] Amphilochius, *On the Sinful Woman*, 1; P.G., 39, 68C.

[5] Severian of Gabala, *On Baptism; P.G.*, 31, 432C.

[6] See H. Rondet, "La croix sur le front", in *R.S.R.*, 42 (1954), p. 392.

into a well, and were miraculously saved because they had a cross painted in red on their foreheads.

Besides the sign of the cross on the brow, it was made on the face. The *Odes of Solomon* and Justin mention this in the second century. A graffito in the Viale Manzoni hypogeum in Rome shows it in the third century.[7] It is attested again in the thirteenth century by Luke of Thuy. There was a parallel development in the big sign of the cross ordinarily used today, from the forehead to the breast and from the left shoulder to the right (at least in the West). But this did not appear before the later Middle Ages, though it may have existed before that as a gesture of blessing or exorcism.

The sign of the cross was a liturgical observance, but it was also depicted as a symbol, on monuments, frescoes, bas-reliefs, mosaics and things of all sorts. In the second and third centuries it appears in the catacombs, both in the Greek form +, and in the Latin form †. But Christians also recognized the cross in various objects whose shape more or less resembles it. Justin notes that it is represented by the mast of a ship with its yard, by the plough, the axe (*ascia*), the military standard (*I Apol.*, 55, 3-4). We have seen that some of these symbols had this meaning in art.

Nowadays the sign of the cross normally calls to mind the gibbet to which Christ was nailed. But we have to ask ourselves whether this was the primary origin of the sign on the forehead in the primitive Christian community. It seems indeed that it was not, that in the beginning it was a matter of a sign that had a different significance. We have to notice that several ancient texts compare the sign of the cross with the letter *tau*, which in Greek had the

[7] J. Carcopino, *De Pythagore aux Apôtres* (Paris, 1956), p. 94.

form T. Examples of this are the *Epistle of Barnabas* (IX, 8) in the second century, and Gregory of Nyssa in the fourth. These texts have been assembled by Father Hugo Rahner.[8]

The bringing together of the cross and *tau* may be accounted for by a resemblance of form. But it is not a very satisfactory resemblance. The Greek *tau*, T, does not agree with the cruciform sign made on the forehead. Something else must be looked for. Now the Fathers of the Church themselves remark that the Book of Ezechiel declares that the members of the messianic community will be marked on their foreheads with the sign *taw*. This text was very much alive in the memory of the Jews in the time of Christ; and the Essenes, who claimed to be the eschatological community, bore the sign of Ezechiel upon their foreheads (*C.D.C.*, XIX, 19).[9]

Furthermore, in the Apocalypse, St John in his turn declares that the elect will be marked on the forehead. We read that the angel prevented the calamities from falling on the world "till we sign the servants of our God in their foreheads" (*Apoc.* 7. 3); and further on (14. 1) the seer sees 144,000 people "having the name of the Lamb and the name of his Father written on their foreheads". This seal (*sphragis*), which is the Father's name, is the sign of Ezechiel. *Taw*, the last letter of the Hebrew alphabet, signifies God, as does the Greek *omega*. Moreover, the rite which John describes has reference to a baptismal usage, as Professor Lampe has shown.[10]

It seems, then, that the first Christians were marked on

8 "Das mystische Tau", in *Z.K.T.*, 75 (1953), pp. 386–410.

9 See J. Daniélou, *The Dead Sea Scrolls and Primitive Christianity* (Baltimore, 1959), pp. 105 ff.

10 *The Seal of the Spirit*, pp. 16–18.

the forehead with a *taw*, which signified the name of
Yahweh. But this raises two questions. In the first place,
are we not faced with the same difficulty over again,
namely, that *taw* is not cross-shaped? But in fact this
apparent difficulty is really a confirmation. For in Christ's
time the *taw* of the Hebrew alphabet was represented by
the sign $+$ or X. It is in this form that we meet it in
Palestinian ossuaries of the first century A.D., and there
we may possibly have the oldest Christian representation
of the cross.[11] It signified the name of Yahweh.

This brings us to the second question: Why should
Christians have borne the sign of Yahweh's name? But
that very expression, "bearing the Name" (of the Lord),
occurs a number of times in an ancient Christian document
marked by Jewish influence, the *Shepherd* of Hermas; and
it is used to denote baptism: "If you bear the Name
without having his power you will be bearing the Name
in vain. The stones which you saw rejected are those who
bore the Name but had not put on the raiment" (*Sim.,*
IX, 13, 2-3). The meaning is clear: whoever is baptized
but does not sanctify himself cannot be saved.

In this passage and in several others the expression
"bearing the Name" certainly appears to denote the fact
of being marked on the forehead with the sign *taw*, that is,
the sign of the cross. Dinkler seeks to verify this in an
interesting way.[12] It looks as if the expression must be
associated with one that we read in the Gospel. Instead of
Matthew's "He that *taketh* not up his cross and followeth
me is not worthy of me" (10. 38), Luke has "Whosoever
doth not *carry* his cross and come after me cannot be my

[11] See B. Bagatti, *art. cit.*, p. 4.
[12] "Jesu Wort vom Kreuztragen", in *Neutestamentliche Studien für
R. Bultmann* (Berlin, 1954), pp. 120-8.

disciple" (14. 27). These words could imply a liturgical allusion to the cross on the forehead.

Nevertheless it remains true that this Christian usage of marking with a sign that denotes the name of Yahweh is a strange one. It disregards the fact that the Name, which in the Old Testament signified the manifestation of God in the world, alongside but independently of God's Word, was for the primitive Christian community a designation of Christ as Word of God incarnate.[13] That is found clearly in the *Shepherd* of Hermas, and also in the *Didache*, where we read: "We thank you, holy Father, for your holy Name which you have made to dwell in our hearts" (x, 2). Here, as Peterson shows, the Name signifies the Word.[14] The *Gospel of Truth*, a second-century homily shot through with Judaeo-Christian theology,[15] is yet more explicit: "Now the Name of the Father is the Son" (38, 5).

It may then be considered sure that the sign of the cross with which the first Christians were marked denoted the name of the Lord, that is to say the Word, and signified that they were consecrated to him. In a Greek environment this symbolism became unintelligible, and the cross was therefore interpreted in another way. In the form + it was regarded as a representation of the instrument of Jesus' suffering; in the form X it was taken for the first letter of Χριστός. But the fundamental idea was unchanged: a consecration of the baptized person to Christ.

So far we have been considering the sign of the cross, in

[13] This is treated more fully in my *Théologie du judéo-christianisme*, pp. 199–216.

[14] "Didachè, cap. 9 et 10", in *E.L.*, 58 (1944), p. 13.

[15] Published in Zurich in 1956 by H. C. Puech, G. Quispel and M. Malinine.

the liturgy and on pictorial monuments, in its simplest form, that of the Greek cross. But as time passed it took on more elaborate forms, especially in archaeology. A study of the subject can be found in the *Dictionnaire d'archéologie chrétienne et de liturgie*, art. Croix, by Dom Henri Leclercq, or in M. Sulzberger's article, "Le Symbole de la croix", in *Byzantion*, 2 (1925), pp. 356–83. I want here to draw attention only to a little-known representation, which is very old and is interesting as combining the cross with the name of Jesus long before he was depicted as crucified.

We may first remark that the association of the cross with the name of Jesus occurs at a very early date in a curious passage of the *Epistle of Barnabas*. The author is discussing the interpretation of the number 318, the number of Abraham's servants. He explains that "18 is written by an *iota*, which stands for 10, and an *eta*, which stands for 8: there you have $IH(\sigma o \tilde{v} s)$" (IX, 8). He then explains that 300 is written by *tau*, which is the cross. So 318 stands both for the cross and the name of Jesus. As regards the last, we have here a first form of that monogram IHS which was to be repeated so often, representing the first three letters of $IHC(o \tilde{v} s)$.

But in very early times the name of Jesus had another symbol, the letter *waw*, for in Greek the name has six letters, and this *waw* was the sixth letter of the alphabet in archaic Greek; it fell into disuse, but kept its place in the list of numbers. The Gnostics speculated on this unusual characteristic. It appears that here again, before the Greek interpretations, there was a Judaeo-Christian basis. A. Dupont-Sommer has demonstrated that the *waw* on an Aramaic Christian *lamella* signified the name of God, that is, Christ.[16]

[16] *La Doctrine gnostique de la lettre waw* (Paris, 1946), p. 34.

Now among the monograms of Christ there is one in which *waw* is associated with the cross. It is found in St Jerome.[17] He is describing a monogram which resembles the ✕, well known on monuments from the third century; and he explains that in the one of which he is thinking the branch coming down from left to right has the form of *waw*, whilst the other two branches are like an *apex* and an *iota*, a traditional figure of the cross. This leads to a sign very like this, ✕. But the most interesting thing is Jerome's interpretation, *waw* joined with the cross. It is very probable that *waw* here denotes the name of Jesus.

This is the more likely because the pattern thus arrived at immediately reminds us of one of the best-known figures which combines Christ and the cross, namely, that of the brazen serpent set up on a pole in the wilderness. Christ himself makes use of this figure: "As Moses lifted up the serpent in the desert, so must the Son of Man be lifted up" (John 3. 14). The serpent is *waw*-shaped, and Justin early gave the form of a cross to the pole (*I Apol.*, LX, 3).

The Fathers often mention this figure, for its source in the New Testament gave it special authority. But it could hardly fail to be a little shocking: how could Christ be represented by a snake? There is an echo of this surprise in Gregory of Nyssa's *Life of Moses* (II, 271–7; S.C., pp. 118–20). It is understandable that justifications should have been sought for this representation. And one of the easiest was to give the serpent the shape of the letter *waw*, the symbol of the name of Jesus. Dupont-Sommer notes that the likeness of *waw* to the shape of the serpent had been one of the reasons for giving the letter a sacred

[17] See G. Morin, "Hieronymus de Monogrammate", in *Rev. Bén.*, 2 (1903), pp. 232–3.

character (*op. cit.*, p. 72). He establishes this for the Hebrew *waw*, and it is true also for the Greek *digamma*. Here again, beneath the Greek interpretations, we reach the ancient level of Aramaic Christianity. And the presence of this sign on Judaeo-Christian ossuaries in Palestine is a striking confirmation of it.[18]

The conclusion reached by our inquiry is this. The sign of the cross is seen to have its origin, not in an allusion to Christ's passion, but as a signification of his divine glory. Even when it comes to be referred to the cross on which he died, that cross is regarded as the expression of the divine power which operates through his death: and the four arms of the cross are looked on as the symbol of the cosmic significance of that redeeming act.

[18] B. Bagatti, *op. cit.*, p. 4.

Index

Date Due

70
71

72
74
75
76
79
80
80